CONSTITUTIONALISM, DEMOCRACY AND SOVEREIGNTY: AMERICAN AND EUROPEAN PERSPECTIVES

UK Association for Legal and Social Philosophy

The UK Association for Legal and Social Philosophy (ALSP) is open to everyone interested in the interaction between theory and practice in the areas of legal, social and political thought; the interplay between these areas; and the applications and outcomes arising out of the inter-disciplinary nature of such debate. In seeking to extend debate beyond the traditional academy, it is especially concerned to include students and practitioners in its activities, as well as to promote discussion with, among and beyond full-time academics.

Membership is currently £20 (waged) or £10 (unwaged) per annum, which includes a subscription to *Res Publica: A Journal of Social and Legal Philosophy* and the Association's newsletter. For details, please write to the Treasurer, Ms P FitzGerald, 7 Adur Court, Stoney Lane, Shoreham-by-Sea, West Sussex BN43 6LY.

Constitutionalism, Democracy and Sovereignty: American and European Perspectives

Edited by

RICHARD BELLAMY
University of Reading

Avebury

Aldershot • Brookfield USA • Hong Kong • Singapore • Sydney

Published by
Avebury
Ashgate Publishing Limited
Gower House
Croft Road
Aldershot
Hants GU11 3HR
England

Ashgate Publishing Company
Old Post Road
Brookfield
Vermont 05036
USA

British Library Cataloguing in Publication Data

Constitutionalism, Democracy and
    Sovereignty: American and European
    Perspectives
    I. Bellamy, Richard
    172

Library of Congress Catalog Card Number: 95-83730

ISBN 185972 264 4

Reprinted 1997

Printed and bound by Athenaeum Press, Ltd.,
Gateshead, Tyne & Wear.

Contents

Section Three: Democracy and the constitution of Europe

Section Four: Constitutionalism beyond the sovereign state

Acknowledgements

These papers were first presented at the 22nd Annual Conference of the UK Association for Legal and Social Philosophy, held at the University of East Anglia from 6–8th April 1995. The editor is very grateful to the officers of the Association, Professor John Bell, Dr Bob Brecher, and Dr Elizabeth Kingdom, and to his UEA colleagues Professor Martin Hollis, Ms Carole Lyons, Dr Tim O'Hagan, Mr Nino Palumbo, Dr Alan Scott and the Politics Sector secretary, Mrs Anne Martin, for their help in organising this event. Vital technological assistance in preparing the manuscript for publication has been provided by Ms Pat FitzGerald, who transformed it into camera-ready copy. The conference formed part of a research project on 'Principles and Languages for the Constitution of Europe' directed by Richard Bellamy and Dario Castiglione, for which they have been awarded an ESRC Project Grant (R000221170).

1 Introduction: Constitutionalism, democracy and sovereignty

Richard Bellamy

Constitutionalism, democracy and sovereignty are both complementary and conflicting terms. At one level, the constitutional desire to subject the exercise of state power to certain normative limits appears to be at odds with both assertions of popular and national sovereignty and the related view that the only legitimate source of law or value lies with the people and the institutions that embody their will. At another level, constitutions may be seen as providing the rules and institutional mechanisms necessary to give expression to that will. For example, many apparent limitations on political power are designed to protect or facilitate the democratic process, such as guarantees of the right to vote and rules of order for debate, whilst others employ the democratic process itself to control the powerful, such as the requirement that office holders seek periodic re-election. Indeed, constitutions themselves are not infrequently the product of democratic struggles or debates and usually contain provisions that allow for their democratic revision or amendment.

This attempted resolution of the paradox of constitutionalism and democracy, however, potentially raises more questions than it answers. By suggesting that constitutions are essentially the artifacts of democracy, it becomes hard to accord them independent weight. Thus, many commentators have insisted that the real constitution of a state lies in its social conditions, culture and political system rather than any formal legal provisions supposedly regulating the exercise of power. After all, the states of the former Communist bloc invariably had written constitutions of an impeccably liberal kind, that offered a highly misleading guide to how their governments actually operated. From this perspective, constitutions are at best the unnecessary adornments of good regimes that work well for totally unrelated reasons, and at worst provide bad regimes with a spurious legitimacy.

In his Austin Lecture, Professor Ulrich Preuss identifies the distinctiveness of modern constitutionalism as the need to reconcile the

1

democratic rule of men with the constitutional rule of law. He argues that constitutional government represents a response to a 'disenchanted' world, in which 'the inherently obligating forces of the Christian–feudal order' have been eroded and replaced by an order based on the natural freedom of individuals and their subjective pursuit of their interests. As he notes, the key difficulty created by this situation was succinctly stated by Madison (1961, p.322) in the *Federalist Papers*: namely, that 'in framing a government which is to be administered by men over men ... you must first enable the government to control the governed; and in the next place oblige it to control itself'. The key lies in combining the rule of men with the rule of law. This project involves both making government operate through laws rather than via arbitrary decisions and ensuring it is itself bound by them.

The paradox of constitutionalism and democracy clearly lies at the heart of this problem. Preuss argues that it cannot be resolved by appealing to higher norms but only through political devices which involve dividing legal authority in ways that allow the people to check themselves. He outlines the three main traditions of constitutionalism and the different ways they have attempted to do just this. Each of these traditions identifies sovereignty and the legitimation of higher law with the people, but not with particular majorities or elected officials. In Britain parliamentary sovereignty can only be expressed through the joint action of all three houses and so, theoretically at least, cannot be identified with the will of the prevailing executive. The American constitution appeals to a founding compact between the people as a whole and claims to speak in their name. The French locate sovereign power in the nation, which exists prior to the constitution rather than being constituted by it, as in the American tradition. The legislature is also subordinate to the national will, although the direct election of the President gives this office its peculiar legitimacy within the system.

Section Two addresses the related topic of whether constitutions prevent radical change by placing all challenges to the established political order beyond the pale of acceptable politics. Critical Legal Studies theorists, for example, maintain that the rule of law is an essentially incoherent notion, since law can be made to mean whatever those in a position to interpret and implement it wish it to. Rights, in particular, are said merely to express personal attitudes, class bias and group or self-interest. As a result, constitutions simply reflect the ideological preferences of those in power. Consequently, these writers believe that constitutionalism and democracy will always be at odds with each other. Law can only cease to be a means of oppression if political and economic power are more equally distributed through the introduction of more participatory forms of decision making (e.g. Tushnet, 1988).

Elizabeth Kingdom and Vivien Hart both dispute this view. They contend that far from constraining political debate and protest, constitutional rights can help motivate and focus demands for change on the part of the oppressed. Kingdom proposes that we should conceive of rights as heuristic devices that serve to direct attention to a specific area of practical politics. She argues that this approach does not entail our seeing rights as logically or temporally prior to political activity, but as emerging through politics as part of the process by which social movements frame a set of questions about strategy and outcome. However, she observes that by formulating their political goals in terms of rights, radical campaigns are broadened from a stance of what Chantal Mouffe has termed 'democratic antagonism' to the prevailing system into a more general 'democratic struggle' for the comprehensive democratisation of social life (Mouffe, 1988, p.96). A strategy of mere antagonism frequently issues in an oppressed or disadvantaged group's pursuing its interests without regard to the impact on similarly placed groups, as when unemployed men blame their condition on immigration or on women entering the labour market. Democratic struggle, in contrast, involves a group's generalising the principles inherent in its demands to take into account the interests of others. The Critical Legal Studies critique of rights and legal discourse proves doubly misplaced, therefore. Not only is it possible for the oppressed to appropriate this language to articulate their own concerns, but in doing so they are not simply dressing up their own narrow interests in legal terms. Rather, the form of law and rights encourages them to adopt a wider and more inclusive perspective.

Vivien Hart suggests that the American campaign for a minimum wage offers a good instance of the employment of rights as heuristics in such a democratic struggle. Comparing the American experience with the parallel policy history in Britain, she argues that the existence of a framework of codified constitutional standards forced both the American activists and the legislature to adopt a more inclusive and open approach than their British equivalents. While in the short run this made the campaign much more protracted, it also rendered the resulting policy more durable and of wider application. Summarising her survey, she comments:

> The logic of the universalism of constitutional promises required the constant justification of differentiation and exclusion and created an expansionist momentum, absent in the fluctuations of British coverage. The constitutional text provided a counter-claim to powerful interests in the political system, to the indifference of political parties and to legislative decisions which the British sweated worker had to accept. Constitutional authority gave standing and legitimacy to the claims of women in the early phase, workers in the middle years and to excluded citizens in the endgame.

Whereas Mrs Thatcher was able to end coverage for young people on pragmatic grounds and with relative ease, the Reagan administration was forced to retreat before the charge of an unjustifiable discrimination on the basis of age.

Hart believes that the development of minimum wage policy in the United States illustrates that a written constitution does not necessarily reinforce the status quo and block radical reforms. In many respects, it has the healthy effect of promoting a principled and universalising tendency within political debate that provides an opening for those whose concerns are being unjustifiably ignored. As a result, she contests the distinction drawn by Bruce Ackerman between a 'normal' politics driven by private or group interests and a 'constitutional' politics that looks to the public good but which only breaks out at exceptional times of national crisis (Ackerman, 1991, Chs. 9–11). Rather, it is possible for normal politics always to possess a constitutional dimension – indeed, this is arguably one of the effects of a country's possessing a constitution.

In the final chapter of this section, John Arthur takes a different tack which is more sympathetic to Ackerman's thesis. He sets out to defend the American practice of judicial review against the charge that it is incompatible with democratic values. He makes three arguments to support his case. First, he points out that the court can play an important role in promoting procedural democratic values of openness and fairness, such as safeguarding the equal right to vote. Second, he argues that even when protecting non-procedural rights, such as those of minorities against majority tyranny, judicial review can be seen as a self-binding pre-commitment on the part of the people themselves, whereby they guard against the possibility of oppressive or misguided laws being passed during normal democratic politics. This argument can be reconciled with democratic values in two ways. It can be seen as resulting from a democratic contract between the whole people – a position that is clearly expressed in the American Constitution's opening claim to speak in the name of 'We the People of the United States'. It can also be said to accord with one of the chief purposes of democratic government, namely the protection of individual rights and justice. Third, Arthur suggests that the special position of judges allows them to deliberate on matters of principle in a more impartial and informed manner than ordinary people or their representatives. Security of tenure and the institutional constraints of the office, such as the requirement that they use legal argument, mean that they are less susceptible to the pressures of interest groups and personal prejudice than politicians or the electorate at large.

These arguments represent an important strand in contemporary defences of constitutionalism. However, all three, and especially the last, are open to criticism for implying the paradoxical belief that ordinary citizens are not fully worthy of the autonomy that provides the main rationale for the very rights judicial review purports to protect. In this respect, a less clear division between constitutional and normal politics, such as the earlier two chapters propose, might be preferred.

4

The issue of whether constitutions matter and if so, in what ways, becomes particularly pertinent in periods of transition. We are currently witnessing, in both Western and Eastern Europe, a remarkable reconfiguration of state and popular sovereignty. In the West, the main pressure for change comes from the European Union and the challenge it poses to the sovereign power of the member states. In the East, political reform stands in an ambiguous relationship to the shift towards capitalist market economies and, in many instances, the redrawing of state boundaries. In both cases, economic change, constitution-making and democratic renewal are occurring simultaneously, although not necessarily at the same pace. However, the degree to which they reinforce each other and the question of whether any one of them ought to be given logical or temporal priority over the others remain matters of fierce debate.

These concerns provide the main focus of the essays in Section Three. Zenon Bankowski and Andrew Scott argue that the creation of the European Union has broken the 'symbiotic relationship' existing between the state, democracy and law. In the traditional understandings of legitimacy and law outlined by Professor Preuss, the rule of law maintains the existence of the state, the state enforces the law and the authority and validation of both law and state rests with the people. European Community law, in contrast, lacks a basis in a European state founded in a European citizenry. Consequently, they maintain, no obvious foundation exists for either the acceptance of, or even the acquiescence to, this law by the people over whom it applies.

Bankowski and Scott examine three proposals that have been canvassed as remedies for this situation. The first suggests that we should simply democratise the institutional structure of the EU, perhaps by strengthening the role of the European Parliament. The second advocates substituting a legal framework based on intergovernmental Treaties with a Constitution that explicitly sets out the aims, and delimits the powers, of the Union – particularly with regard to such matters as citizenship. Finally, the third looks to the emergence of a collective EU identity possessing all the characteristics and symbolism associated with nation states.

In their view, none of these proposals proves satisfactory. Following Joseph Weiler (1992), they argue that although the first two might provide the Union with a formal legitimacy, they fail to tackle the real problem of social legitimacy. The third, in contrast, somewhat begs the issue, since the very problem and challenge of the European Union derives from the fact that it cannot either theoretically or practically be conceived simply as the nation state writ large. Their suggestion is that law needs to be seen in a polycentric way as a set of interacting and interlocking normative and territorial systems. This approach is fluid enough not to breach the pillars of the prevailing nation state order, but firm enough to bind them together around the four central economic freedoms of the Union and to provide the associated system of law with legitimation.

5

Arguably, the establishment of European Citizenship in Article 8 of the Treaty of European Union marks the start of official recognition of the legitimation issue and is an attempt to address it. Unfortunately, as Carole Lyons shows in her chapter, it offers little that is new. Many of the rights granted in Article 8 already existed as a result of earlier Treaties. More importantly, citizenship of the EU is made dependent on being a national of one of the member states. This decision fails to grapple with the major differences in defining nationality that exist between these countries, and leaves the 10–15 million non-national residents within the Union, such as Turkish workers in Germany, disenfranchised. In these ways, this new citizenship serves more to buttress existing national identities and to exclude non-nationals than it does to build popular allegiance to European institutions.

In the last chapter of this section, Richard Bellamy and Dario Castiglione extend this discussion of the changing relationship between national sovereignty, constitutional arrangements and democratic accountability to Eastern Europe as well as the EU. They contend that economic success cannot be counted on to endow either the Union or the new regimes of Eastern Europe with legitimation. Rather, political mechanisms are required. Returning to Weiler's (1992) distinction between formal and social legitimacy, they argue that whilst a cosmopolitan-orientated constitutionalism centred on human rights might provide the first, it needs to be complemented by a communitarian form of democracy to achieve the second. As a result, they follow Bruce Ackerman (1992) in advocating the need for a constitutional politics to motivate popular support for the political changes in East and West Europe. However, they also believe that we must adopt a more political approach to constitutional design. In addition to the usual negative Madisonian checks that can be introduced through devices such as bicameral legislatures, this political constitutionalism emphasises the positive role played by democratic politics in giving people a say in the framing and maintenance of the legal order governing their lives.

The need to rethink the relationship between law and state sovereignty is at the centre of the whole European debate. In the final section of this volume, Elspeth Attwooll and Luigi Ferrajoli insist that we ought to divorce the two completely and go beyond the sovereign state. Attwooll shows how neither the domestic law of Britain nor international law can adequately accommodate the demands of a significant number of Scots for self-determination. The reason lies in a tendency within both to identify popular sovereignty with the sovereignty of existing states. Instead, she suggests that we need to prioritise the first and give due weight to group identity at the substate level.

Professor Ferrajoli goes further. He argues that state sovereignty and citizenship are totally at odds with the concepts of law and human rights respectively. Sovereign power involves the authority to act outside the law.

6

According to this doctrine, might is right. By associating rights with a certain type of membership of a particular state, citizenship denies their universality. Within states these contradictions are liable to go unnoticed. It is primarily in their relations with other states that governments feel authorised to acknowledge no law. It is with regard to non-nationals that citizenship warrants excluding certain individuals or groups from the rights protection that ought to be accorded to all human beings.

Ferrajoli contends that the process of globalisation has rendered this distinction between the domestic character of states and their external aspect increasingly hard to sustain. A global economy has enhanced job mobility across national borders, leading to mass migration to the richer economies and demands from non-nationals that their work and living conditions be regulated according to the same standards as those of citizens. National policies to regulate pollution, the flow of capital, defence, production and employment defence – in sum all the standard tasks of government – have become to a large extent untenable. Cooperation with other states is unavoidable, with the result that multinational organisations in the areas of trade, information, finance and armed conflict have become increasingly important, thereby eroding state sovereignty. Law is no exception to this development. In particular, Ferrajoli believes that the United Nations Charter of 1945 and the Universal Declaration of Human Rights of 1948 provide the basis for a global constitutionalism that essentially undercuts the legitimacy of sovereignty and citizenship. He concludes that the task for the future is to provide the institutional instruments capable of making these new legal principles operable. As the European Union reveals, this task will not be easy and will almost certainly be resisted by nation states at first – an analysis borne out by the findings of the second section. Nor is it clear that law can be disassociated from sovereignty so easily if it is to retain popular legitimacy. Many analysts have maintained, for example, that a global constitutionalism would necessitate a cosmopolitan system of democracy and possibly a world state (Held, 1992) In which case, the tension between democracy, sovereignty, and constitutionalism, that acts both to promote and to threaten law and rights, is likely to remain.

Notes

1 I am grateful to Dario Castiglione for his comments on an earlier version of this introduction.

7

References

Ackerman, B. (1991), *We the People: Foundations*, Vol. I, Harvard University Press: Cambridge, Mass.

Ackerman, B. (1992), *The Future of Liberal Revolution*, Yale University Press: New Haven and London.

Madison, J. (with Hamilton, A. and Jay, J.) (1961), *The Federalist Papers*, first edition 1788, Rossiter, C. (ed.), New York University Press: New York.

Held, D. (1992), 'Democracy: from city-states to a cosmopolitan order?' in id. (ed.), *Prospects for Democracy, Political Studies*, Special Issue, 40, pp.10–39.

Mouffe, C. (1988), 'Hegemony and new political subjects: toward a new concept of democracy' in Nelson, C. and Grossberg, L. (eds.), *Marxism and the Interpretation of Culture*, University of Illinois Press: Urbana and Chicago.

Weiler, J.H.H. (1992), 'After-Maastricht: Community Legitimacy in Post-1992 Europe' in Adams, W.J. (ed.), *Singular Europe: Economy and Polity of the European Community after 1992*, University of Michigan Press: Ann Arbor.

Tushnet, M. (1988), *Red, White and Blue: A Critical Analysis of Constitutional Law*, Harvard University Press: Cambridge, Mass.

Section One
AUSTIN LECTURE

2 The political meaning of constitutionalism

Ulrich K. Preuss

Constitutionalism – a thriving concept

Constitutionalism is one of the few political ideas which have apparently escaped the general suspicion cast upon most of the other prominent 'isms' in the last decade. Perhaps one may even say that constitutionalism has risen to the status of the only contemporary political idea that enjoys almost universal acceptance. In the last 20 years, a considerable number of countries in different geographical regions with extremely diverse conditions have concurrently chosen the path to constitutionalism in order to find a way out of their respective quandaries: be it Argentina, Brazil, Paraguay and Uruguay in Latin America; Portugal, Spain and Greece at the Southern rim of Europe; South Africa; or Russia and the post-communist countries of Eastern and Central Europe – all of them (and several others) have regarded constitutionalism as the basic objective which sets the framework for their further economic, social, cultural, and political development. No less important is the envisioned role of constitutionalism for the project of European integration. There is a broadening consensus among the citizens of the EU Member States that a common market and more or less remote European institutions in Bruxelles, Strasbourg and Luxembourg will no longer suffice to sustain the aspiration of a European Union. Not accidentally, the idea of a European Polity – for some people a threat, for others a promise – has been associated with the quest for a European constitution. For in Europe the concept of a polity has been intimately linked with the idea of constitutionalism since the end of the 18th century.

All this conveys strong indications of the vitality of the idea of constitutionalism. It may even be justified to credit constitutionalism with certain economic achievements. A comparative view of the present political world system reveals that constitutional democracies enjoy relatively robust economies and have been relatively successful in the

11

domestication of class cleavages and in coping with other social conflicts. Moreover, despite the tendency of the industrial societies to overuse scarce natural resources and to pursue relentlessly the principle of efficient resource allocation, the average standard of environmental protection is higher in traditional constitutional states than in countries with authoritarian political systems. To be sure, these are correlations, not necessarily causal explanations, and there are exceptions. On the one hand, we know of constitutional states which suffer from serious economic difficulties, great social inequalities and severe religious and ethnic cleavages and yet have firmly resisted the temptation to lapse into authoritarianism. India is certainly the most prominent example. On the other hand, countries like Taiwan, South Korea, Singapore and nowadays also China take pride in the rapid economic development which they achieved in frameworks of government which have maintained, to say the least, large distances from the essentials of constitutionalism.

When we speak of constitutionalism, we refer to the set of ideas and principles which form the common basis of the rich variety of constitutions which we find in many countries of the world. Roughly speaking, constitutionalism includes the key tenets of a polity which is based on the idea that the ruled are not merely passive objects of the rulers' willpower but have the status of active members of the political community. This relation entails certain bonds of mutuality between the rulers and the ruled which form the constitution. Thus, constitutionalism encompasses institutional devices and procedures which determine the formation, structure and orderly functioning of government, and it embodies the basic ideas, principles, and values of a polity which aspires to give its members a share in the government. This basket of ideas is fairly impressive and would certainly do the most excellent political philosophers much credit. However, it does not grasp the distinctiveness of constitutionalism. This is not to be found in certain ideas or institutional devices, ingenious as they may be, like, for example, the idea of the separation of powers, or the conception of the accountability of the rulers *vis-à-vis* the ruled; the essence of constitutionalism which has prompted both the admiration and the constant reasoning of the most spirited political philosophers of many centuries is the mystery of its binding force.

Several political philosophers have developed ideas about how to conceive of a good polity in which the rulers are benevolent and work for the best interests of the ruled, or in which the rulers have certain duties *vis-à-vis* their subjects. Moreover, long before the age of modern constitutionalism, we find many examples of compacts in which a ruler enters into binding promises and guarantees *vis-à-vis* his or her subjects. This is not constitutional government in the modern sense of the term. Constitutionalism in this sense is the response to two conditions of modernity: first, the emergence of a monistic sovereign state power after the downfall of the balance between secular and ecclesiastic authority characteristic of mediaeval society; and, second, the idea of the natural freedom of the individual who creates his or her obligations by virtue of his or her interests. Constitutionalism is the answer to the erosion of the inherently obligating forces of the Christian–feudal order and its transformation into an order based on the subjectivity of individuals' interests. In the evolving modern world of the 16th and 17th centuries, one torn by religious cleavages and civil wars, sovereign power became the guarantor of peace and order. At the same time, only the power which could be derived from the natural freedom of the individual was legitimate. Constitutionalism is the conception of a polity in which sovereign power and natural individual freedom coexist and create a political order which cannot resort to antecedent bonds of mutual obligation but must produce its very own mechanisms of obligations. Constitutionalism is, in other words, the answer to the horrifying experience that worldly rule has become immanent; that is, that naturally free individuals have to create a good order by their own limited means. The main problem of this difficult task is the construction of a device in which the sovereign and unlimited power of the united individuals is subjected to the restraining force of legally binding rules. In fact, the legal form of government which rejects the idea of any kind of pre-legal power is the main feature and the great achievement of modern constitutionalism.

The constitution as a law

When I speak of the quality of the constitution as a law I refer to two characteristics. The first is the positivity of modern law. Positive law is the term for that kind of law which owes its authority and binding force not to its religious, philosophical or otherwise sacred content, nor to its tradition, but to its origin from a legitimate lawgiver (see Weber, 1978, Ch. VIII, Sect. VII, pp.866ff). The law has become a function of the lawgiver's power and will, and in order to motivate the obedience of the ruled it need not refer to its immanent qualities and teleology, but relies on its formal–procedural quality as the result of a more or less arbitrary enactment. This is the essence of Thomas Hobbes' (1841, p.202) famous statement that not the inherent truth, but the authority of the author provides the binding force of the law – 'auctoritas, non veritas facit legem'. It is also the hallmark of positivity.

The second property of modern law consists in the separation of morality from legality. This means the institutionalisation of obedience without the invocation of any moral grounds on which the law may, or may not, be based. Modern law encompasses and obligates all members of society, irrespective of their moral, religious, or political convictions. This makes it possible to bind them together under a common law even if, which is likely to be the case, they do not share the same religious beliefs, philosophical values or historical traditions.

These two properties of modern law allow for the enactment and change of law on mere grounds of expediency according to changing circumstances. Since in modern societies circumstances change rapidly it is justified to say that the positivist and demoralised character of modern law implies the institutionalisation of legal changes and, by virtue of this, the abstraction from social relations which are integrated by commonly shared values (Luhmann, 1972, pp.209 and *infra*). As Polanyi stated for the market, so we can speak of a high degree of disembeddedness of modern law in relation to other institutions of society.

What is the implication of the legal form of the constitution? What does it mean to say that the legitimation, limitation and regulation of political power assumes the form of legality, i.e., that the obligatory character of the rules which authorise, bind, limit and make political power accountable does not emanate from the inherent dignity of the values and principles which 'govern the governor', but instead from its enactment by a legitimate lawgiver? Does this presuppose a lawgiving authority superior to the ruler which itself has to be bound? This assumption would be self-contradictory. Constitutionalism does not cast out the devil by means of Beelzebub: it does not limit the sovereign power of the lawmaking authority by superimposing a super-sovereign power on it. Only God could rightfully claim this place, but it was the erosion of the undisputed authority of His commands that engendered the secularisation of the concept of supreme power in the first place. Obviously the idea of a super-sovereign would not be the solution of the problem, but its mere displacement.

How then to solve the problem of binding the absolutist sovereign power by means of law without relapsing into the idea of a transcendent power to which could be attributed the capacity of imposing its commands on the secular power? How could one possibly conceive of a source of authority which issued laws that were able to bind the sovereign ruler without transforming this authority into a super-sovereign ruler which now in its turn had to be bound? Does not this question lead us unfailingly into a logical impasse? The answer which shifts the problem onto a new theoretical level is the famous demand: for the 'rule of laws and not of men'. From an analytical perspective, the development proceeded in two steps.

The first developmental step towards the constitutional concept of the rule of law meant: the arbitrary and discretionary will power of the ruling person is substituted by the requirement that the government rule *through* laws (Gaus, 1994, p.329). Acts of domination must acquire the form of the law. Obviously this principle makes sense only if the law has qualities which distinguish it from the mere will of the sovereign. This was the claim of the anti-absolutists. Just as the laws of nature reflected the inherent rationality, predictability and immutability of the world – laws which even the Deists' God Himself could not manipulate at will – so a law which imposed its binding force on individuals and which they had the moral duty to obey had to have similar qualities. A law must be a rule, i.e., it must be general (as opposed to an individual order of the sovereign), and it must be immutable in order to be immune from the arbitrariness and vacillations of the power holder. The law is the institutional expression of the continuity, calculability and predictability of the social world; it is the embodiment of reason which checks the passions of the ruler (Jellinek, 1919, pp.43ff).

The underlying idea of the requirement that a law be abstract and general was the claim that what was binding for all should be the embodiment of universally valid truths and at the same time reflect the spirit of the whole polity, not just of particular segments or individual persons. The form of the law domesticates the will power of the sovereign ruler and thus forces it to exercise its power in a reasonable manner. Essentially, the law is not will, but reason; not *voluntas*, but *ratio*. This is the first step towards the conclusion that the law-giving authority must be vested in a body which is qualified for issuing general rules, i.e., which in some way represents the spirit of the whole body politic.

However, this first step did not yet mean the full attainment of constitutionalism. While the requirements of the rule *through* law forced the absolutist monarch to employ the form of the law for all acts which applied to all his or her subjects, it is not at all clear how this requirement could itself acquire the binding force of a law. The difficulty was succinctly stated by Madison (1961, p.322):

> If angels were to govern men, neither external nor internal controls on government would be necessary. In framing a government which is to be administered by men over men, the great difficulty lies in this: you must first enable the government to control the governed; and in the next place oblige it to control itself.

The full elaboration of this idea is nothing less than the invention of the concept of constitutionalism.

As I stated, the rule of law in the variant of the rule *through* law contains no inherent guarantee that the law's rationalising potential will unfold. Only if the obligation of the ruler to employ the form of the law for his or her acts of rule is itself an obligation of the law can we speak of a constitutional rule. Hence, the rule of law has a twofold meaning: rule *through* law and rule *by* law (Gaus, 1994, p.329): acts of domination must acquire the form of the law (government *through* law), and the government itself subjects its will power to the constraints of the law (rule *by* law). This latter element originates in the last analysis in what the famous English mediaeval jurist Henry de Bracton had already stated in the 13th century with great clarity: the king does not make the law, the law makes the king – not 'rex facit legem, lex facit regem' (de Bracton, 1968, pp.33, 306, quoted in Bridge, 1995). In Britain, where absolutism was defeated in its early stages, the 'law-makes-the-king' doctrine gave rise to the constitutional theory that the power to make laws rested in the polity as a whole, not in any single part of it, and that the binding force of the laws followed from the consensus of all of its parts. As Richard Hooker (Jellinek, 1919, p.48) put it, a legislative power of the king which was not authorised by the constitution but exercised in his own right was tantamount to tyranny.

From a jurist's conceptual perspective, one of the main questions of constitutionalism is how to establish a legal obligation of the lawmaker him- or herself without violating sound principles of jurisprudential reasoning. At first glance, the legalisation of lawmaking – i.e., the subjection of the lawgiver and his or her actions to the rules of the law – seems to presuppose a legal hierarchy: one is led to assume that the law which stipulates the requirements for the enactment of a law must have a higher authority than the enacted law itself. However, this would force us to surmise a hierarchy of lawgiving authorities, with the truly supreme authority of the ruler who makes the rules about lawmaking at the top, and the derived authority of the lawmaker proper who is bound by the rules of the supreme power below. This hierarchical concept of law forces us to find a source of law which is superior to the sovereign law giver, and even this 'super-sovereign' must be ruled by a super-super-sovereign because, according to this hierarchical logic, his or her right to make rules for the sovereign must in turn be based on a superior law. This drives us into an infinite regression. In fact, the creative invention of constitutionalism is different.

From a sociological perspective, the legalisation of lawmaking is but one example of a more general social practice which Luhmann (1972, 1974, pp.32ff, 213ff) has termed 'reflexive mechanisms'. We speak of reflexivity when a particular process is applied to itself: the learning of learning, the research on research, the talking over talk, or the making of rules for rule making are examples for reflexive mechanisms. (Evidently H.L.A. Hart's secondary rules – rules about the making, unmaking and the validity of legal rules – are the result of reflexive mechanisms.) Two particularities of reflexivity are of special interest for our topic: first, it increases the range of options which are available in a society in that it allows for selection from among the huge bulk of possible actions. If I learn how to learn I do not have to learn everything that might be important – I gain the freedom to select what I need to learn in the different situations of life. Likewise, if a society makes rules over rule making it increases its capacity for rule making in that it creates and maintains the – more and more professionalised – knowledge about how, when and to what degree a matter should be regulated by law, and thus enhances the power to select among several possibilities.

The second property of reflexivity in our field of law is the surprising instance that in order to establish rules about rule making it is not necessary to establish a hierarchy of legal norms such that rules about how to enact rules and how to establish their validity etc. are superior to the laws which regulate substantive matters. This would finally amount to the idea of a government of angels over people, whereas the problem is the government of people over people whereby 'all men are created equal'. Rousseau (1968, Bk. 2, Ch. 7, p.84) had analysed the problem in a manner very similar to that of the Federalists: In order to find the best rules of society,

> there would need to exist a superior intelligence, who could understand the passions of men without feeling any of them, who had no affinity with our nature but knew it to the full, whose happiness was independent of ours, but who would nevertheless make our happiness his concern... .

Rather than establishing an ultimate source of authority which controls the ruler by virtue of its superior power and authority, constitutionalism imagines a non-hierarchical order in which the single one and undivided state authority is divided into different functions which in turn are distributed among institutionalised branches of state authority. The separation of powers, which Article 16 of the French Declaration declared an indispensable element of any constitution, is indeed essential for constitutionalism, in that it establishes a rule which 'governs the governor' without resorting to the obvious idea of a monistic supreme authority which controls the governor and which therefore operates as the ultimate guarantor of an orderly political rule. The characteristic of constitutionalism is a horizontal order of state authority, in which a system of careful coordination of the functionally specified powers produces a web of mutual and almost circular dependence whereby either one state power can only act on the antecedent action of another or it is subject to subsequent scrutiny and, if need be, censure.

Although the essential property of constitutionalism is the quality of constitutions as a law, this does not mean that the source of legal authority is alike for all constitutions. In fact, I contend that the typologies and distinctions which have been offered in the long history of constitutional reasoning originate in the final analysis in different conceptions about the source of the legally binding force of the respective constitutions. Be it the distinction between written and unwritten constitutions; between rigid and flexible; between those which are more fundamental than ordinary laws (whatever this may mean) and those which have the status of ordinary law; between constitutions which can be amended by the ordinary legislature and those whose revision requires an exclusive amending authority, or the distinction between juridically and politically enforceable constitutions – all these distinctions aim at the clarification of the source and legitimation of the authority of the constitution in its quality as a law. Needless to say, probably the most debated questions of constitutionalism – the questions of who are the authoritative interpreters of the constitution and which methods have to be employed (Murphy, 1993, pp.3–25) – lie at the core of this basic problem.

Patterns of constitutional authority

In the third part of this lecture I want to give a brief account of three patterns of constitutional authority representing different versions of constitutionalism. Incidentally, they have also proven to be the most influential concepts in the last 300 years.

The British constitutional tradition

The British concept of constitutionalism is clearly the most traditional one and at the same time the one whose particular solution of the problem of the authority of the constitution is least transferable to other societies. At first glance it seems paradoxical to understand the doctrine of parliamentary sovereignty as the embodiment of the British concept of constitutionalism – after all, is not the negation of an unbound sovereign power the essence of constitutionalism? Does not constitutionalism require that the sovereign power, whoever may be its holder, be subject to the constitution? The British version of constitutionalism's answer to this question is rather complex. It rearranges the vertical problem of a hierarchical order, i.e., of supremacy and subordination, into a horizontal problem of coordinating and balancing different parts of the sovereign power: the Parliament consists of three elements; it is, strictly speaking, the Queen in Parliament, including the monarch, the House of Commons and the House of Lords. They are sovereign only through common action, and being bound to each other by mutual rights and duties, the concept of sovereignty acquires a meaning entirely inconsistent with that developed by Bodin (1962) or Hobbes (1991): while they conceived of it as an absolute, undivided and unbound power, in the concept of British constitutionalism it is instituted in a web of cooperative relations of the three constituents of Parliament. They can exercise their sovereign power only in joint action, and this gives rise to the complementary element of British constitutionalism, namely the doctrine of the rule of law.

Rule of law does *not* mean the supremacy of abstract legal principles over the sovereign – this would raise the logically and practically unsolvable problem of a sovereign superior to the sovereign; as I stated earlier, it signifies that the Parliament (always to be understood in its three constituents) can exercise its sovereign power only *through* law. For British subjects the 'rule of law' means the absence of 'arbitrariness, of prerogative, or even of wide discretionary authority on the part of the government' (Dicey, 1915, p.120). Moreover, when the British invoke the 'rule of law' they do not think of abstract principles or of an enumeration of individual rights insured to them by some supreme power, but of the existence of remedies and courts which protect their freedoms – *ubi jus ibi remedium* (Dicey, 1915, p.118). The law exists, as it were, in the operation of the courts which protect the citizens against any kind of wrongdoings which he or she might suffer from the government or a private person. In other words, the authority of the law which binds the government – that is, the 'law of the constitution' – does not derive from a supreme power, least of all from the sovereignty of Parliament, but from the operation of those institutions which secure the exercise of the individuals' freedoms. Note that this idea presupposes that 'there is an area of freedom into which the law should not intervene other than to ensure that the freedom is guaranteed' (Bridge, 1995, p.1). The rights to individual freedom are not created by the law, i.e., derived from principles of the law, but, as Dicey put it, they are 'inherent in the ordinary law of the land' in that they flow from the remedies which the British are granted by the Courts. Thus, in Britain, 'the law of the constitution is little else than a generalisation of the rights which the Courts secure to individuals', or, put conversely, the rights of individuals are part of the constitution because they are inherent elements of the ordinary course of the law of the land (Dicey, 1915, p.119). From this it follows that Dicey is quite right to state that, due to the embeddedness of individual rights in the institutional web of the law of the land, 'the right is one which can hardly be destroyed without a thorough revolution in the institutions and manners of the nation' (Dicey, 1915, p.120). If this still holds true in our day it would mean that in order to suspend or do away with certain rights it would seem necessary to destroy entire entrenched institutions, which in the end may do more harm to the country than the cancellation of a single right by way of a revision of a written constitution. Or, to put it in a more pointed manner, in order to change the constitution the British must make a revolution, because the binding authority of their constitution is not freely disposable to an identifiable single actor, and its alteration is not subject to legally defined procedures. Thus, the constitution of Britain is very much the result of its political culture and not the emanation of one single authoritative source. Its legal quality is derived from the ordinary course of the law of the land, quite the opposite of the continental concepts of constitutionalism which teach that the validity and authority of the law is derived from the constitution. Not surprisingly, in Britain the idea of the constitution as embodied in one written document has never gained a foothold.

The American constitutional tradition

As we know, in sharp contrast to Britain, the character of the constitution as a written text has become one of the hallmarks of the American concept of constitutionalism. Its other distinctive feature is the constitution's status as a supreme law. Of course, the written form is by no means a mere formality. In fact, it is as essential to the authority and validity of the constitution as is the textual embodiment of God's spirit and word in Holy Scripture (Grey, 1984). The written text is the solemn expression of the mutual promises and obligations of the citizens who by this very act constitute a polity among themselves – it is, as Hannah Arendt (1973, pp.169–73) put it, the result of a horizontal social contract which creates mutually binding legal obligations. The written form is the almost sacred affirmation of these promises. As Thomas Paine (1979, p.209) wrote about the constitutions of the states which they had enacted before forming the United States of America, in each state that constitution served, 'not only as an authority, but as a law of control to the government. It was the political bible of the state'.

Evidently the authority derived from its legally binding character and that emanating from its quasi-biblical scriptural form merge and support the other feature of the US constitution, namely its character as a supreme law. Supreme law means that all branches of government, including the legislature itself are the creatures of the constitution. This constitution is, as Thomas Paine (1979, pp.210, 213) put it, 'a thing antecedent to the government', originating from a compact 'of the people with each other, to produce and constitute a government'. More striking than the priority of the constitution over the government is its priority over the will of the people itself – the US constitution is clearly supposed to restrain and even to thwart the will of the majority. This is why time and again constitutionalism and democracy have been regarded as opposites, the term constitutional democracy verging on an oxymoron (see, e.g., Holmes, 1988).

I do not want to pursue this matter but, rather, to deal with the slightly different question of how the constitution can acquire the status of a law which is able to impose its superior authority on its own creator, the people. An obvious answer is the theory of self-binding, the so-called Ulysses strategy – the people protect themselves against their own potential myopia, passions, ignorance etc. This is a functional explanation which gives no reason how it is possible that the constitution is the supreme law and can bind not only the government, but even its own creator.

The answer is somewhat surprising. When we look for a justification of the supremacy of the constitution we are inclined to reason within a hierarchical framework, e.g., in Kelsen's theory of a hierarchy of the legal order. But despite the rhetoric of 'supreme law', which indeed suggests a hierarchical order, the supremacy of the constitution derives from neither of the sources which we have dealt with thus far, i.e., neither from an authority which claims superiority over the people – this is an obvious impossibility – nor from its 'immanent and teleological qualities' (Weber, 1978, p.867), nor from its merely traditional character as originating in venerable old times which might convey to the constitution its superiority over all other laws. Rather, its quasi-sacred character emanates from its feature as a mutual promise of individuals who enter into a compact with each other by which they transform themselves into a nation; which means that they pledge to each other to stay together in a common polity in good and in bad times (Murphy, 1993, p.9). It is the sanctity of the *founding act* by which the polity has been created which imputes to the constitution the authority of the supreme law. The supremacy of its authority over all other laws flows from the inherent significance and uniqueness of the act of nation building. The essential constitutional question which arises is how to preserve the legacy of the founding act, i.e., how to keep the polity alive. Is it more appropriate (and more loyal to the ideas of the founders) to stick to the letter of their sacred scripture in which their original intentions are best determined, or does the sanctity of the founding act require an adjustment of the founders' inspirations to the conditions of the contemporary world? The locus of this debate is the field of constitutional interpretation. Is the *text* of the constitution, the written embodiment of the founders' intentions, the supreme authority, or is it the contemporary *context* which gives the text its particular and, depending on circumstances, changing meaning, so that the constitution is the object of an ever changing struggle about its appropriate interpretation and implementation?

Whatever the right answer may be, the supremacy of the constitution is, in any case, presupposed not only over all branches of government, but also over the people themselves. This is the genuinely American spirit of constitutionalism: the making of the constitution is the act of founding the nation, and whatever purposes, aspirations, hopes, fears, achievements, disappointments, traumas and tragedies of the nation through its eventful history may have occurred or may arise in the future, it is the constitution from which the people will try to extract the right answers to their questions. That is the ultimate reason for the almost obsessive passion of

21

American scholars, lawyers, politicians and great parts of the general public for questions of constitutional interpretation. Incidentally, the other obsession is with rights. Charles Taylor (1992, p.429) has drawn our attention to the slightly aggressive character of American political life and its 'culture of rights', which underscores the 'value on energetic, direct defence of rights' (cf. Lacey and Haakonssen, 1992). Not surprisingly, in this culture the main guarantor of individuals' rights are the courts. The people living under a constitution whose Bill of Rights starts with the prohibition 'Congress shall make no law ...' would certainly sense it as a mere perversity if they should regard the legislature as the defender of their rights rather than as the main source of their endangerment.

The French constitutional tradition

This rights-protecting and -engendering role of parliament is, in fact, one of the characteristics of the French model of constitutional authority. It is neither based on the rootedness of the law in the institutions which protect individuals against arbitrary rule nor on the sacredness of a founding act of nation building which is embodied in a written document. The French concept of constitutionalism is deeply rooted in the idea of the sovereignty of the constituent power and its logical priority over the constituted powers. This opposition explains the striking feature of French constitutional history and theory: that despite the importance which the idea of the constitution has gained during the Great French Revolution, the concept of an eternal, paramount, or supreme law never arose.

The legal authority of French constitutions has been considerably lower than that of the US since their revolutionary origination in 1789 and 1791 respectively (Henkin, 1989). The idea that the constitution is the supreme law to which all branches of government, including the Parliament and the President, are subordinated never gained a foothold in France. Until our day the French concept of constitutionalism has not embraced the institution of judicial review, i.e., the control of the constitutionality of an enacted law through the judiciary.[1] The arbiter in disputes over the interpretation of the constitution between the different branches of government is neither a Court nor the Constitutional Council, but the popularly elected President of the Republic who symbolises the unity and integrity of the Nation. Most surprisingly, the constitution of the homeland of the famous and globally influential and venerated Declaration of the Rights of Man and Citizen does not even include an explicit bill of rights. Its pre-amble contains a solemn proclamation of 'attachment' to the Rights of Man as they were defined in the Declaration of 1789, but this does not mean its legally binding incorporation into the constitution. To the contrary, Article 34 of the constitution explicitly states that the civil rights of the citizens and the guarantees for the exercise of their political freedoms will be taken care of by *law*.

In other words, when the French look for a guardian of their rights and their political freedom, they point to the parliament, not to the courts. The parliament is not viewed, as in the US, as a potential threat to individuals' rights against which the courts must be invoked, but as the guarantor of their realisation. In the French constitutional tradition the idea of political freedom has been inherently connected with the concept of the general will, which in the last analysis refers to the idea of collective redemption and to the belief in the inherent equality of all people before God. Evidently this basically Catholic doctrine stands in stark contrast to Protestant individualism. Consequently, French constitutional doctrine has always been much more concerned with the integrity of the collective will of the nation than about the rights of the individual.

What, then, is the political meaning of constitutionalism in the French tradition? On what does the authority of the constitution rest, and how can its binding force be explained? The answers are not easily found, but a few hypotheses offer themselves. First, the genuine spirit of constitutionalism and its binding force is not encapsulated in the *constitution* but in the *constituent power* of the nation. The constituent power is the creator of all constituted powers and cannot itself be bound by the constitution. The constitution is neither the source of political freedom nor of political integration, much less of political inspiration. All these purposes are embodied in the idea of the nation rather than in the notion of constitutionalism. Unlike the United States, the creation of the constitution has not been the founding act for the French nation – rather, the constitution is one of the emanations of the nation. The nation is antecedent to the constitution. True, there is also in the French version of constitutionalism a mythical founding act, but this is the act of founding the *nation*, i.e., of creating the constituent power which subsequently produces a constitution. This constitution cannot and must not bind its creator, that is, the nation itself. In the words of Emmanuel Joseph Sieyès (1963, pp.124, 126–28): 'The nation is prior to everything. It is the source of everything. Its will is always legal; indeed, it is the law itself'. Therefore the nation cannot be subject to the constitution.

The essence of this concept of constitutionalism, then, is not embodied in the constitution itself; it is incarnated in the power of the nation to make and unmake a constitution at will and at any time. Constitutionalism, that is, consists of what one might call, 'constitution-creativity'; the potential of the nation to constitute and reconstitute its sovereign power and give it its appropriate institutional shape at will. This dynamic idea of constitutionalism accounts for many of the particularities which we encounter in the French tradition, for example, the comparatively large number of French constitutions in the last two centuries, or the relatively weak differentiation between ordinary laws and the constitution in terms of their legally binding force. As in the US, the idea of supremacy is there; but, unlike in the US, it is not associated with the idea of the constitution, but with the pre-constitutional notion of the constituent power of the nation. In fact, the constitution is the embodiment of an inferior rather than of a superior political and legal authority.

Some preliminary conclusions

This sketchy account of the three main traditions of constitutionalism (which are of course by no means exhaustive) shows the difficulty of conceiving a clear cut, unambiguous and undisputed idea of constitutionalism. This is, of course, not very surprising, since the concept is supposed to deliver the answer to one of the most intricate problems of political philosophy, namely the 'governance of the government'. Neither Plato's idea of the rule of the philosophers, nor premodern conceptions of the ruler as the worldly proxy of a Deity, or as the Vicar of Christ, can any longer, if they ever could, provide a solution to this problem in a world of immanence in which the normatively binding force of (moral or legal) obligations can only be established by inner-worldly mechanisms. When, in the 16th and 17th centuries, the traditional conceptions of the good and the right had been eroded and become radically pluralised, the idea of authority and governance had to be reformulated in as radical a manner. Not only the modern monistic concept of sovereignty, but its conceptual and normative foundation in the subjectivity of the governed required, but at the same time also facilitated, the conception of a political authority with which the rulers were entrusted and hence did not possess in their own right. The legal codification of this relation between the governors and the governed, who are conceived as parts of an overarching common polity, is the basic idea of constitutionalism. The quality of constitutions as laws, i.e., as generating the *legal* obligations of the governors, is essential. Only if the bond between the governors and the governed obligates the ruler, irrespective of his or her personal qualities, religious beliefs or else normative convictions, and if it cannot be revoked unilaterally by the ruler, is it possible to form a reliable institutional structure of government in which the governed are recognised as the ultimate source of political authority.

These are the common traits of any concept of constitutionalism. However, the answers to the question of how this authority is institutionalised and rendered a permanent element of the polity so that the government is effectively bound are quite different: while the British concept relies very much on the operation of deeply entrenched institutions which permeate through the social texture (the three elements of Parliament, its rule through and by law, and the remedy-engendering operation of the Courts), both the American and the French notions presuppose one single locus in which the source of the authority of the constitution is embodied. In the case of the US it is the charisma of the founding act which is to be preserved over history in the text of the constitution and which makes this document a legacy, sometimes perhaps a burdensome legacy of the past which imposes itself on future generations. Knowing that this original compact of the Founding Fathers cannot be repeated, all its solemnity and pathos is 'invested' into the text of the constitution. Not accidentally, an American author uses the image of a 'marriage consummated through the pledging partners' positive, active consent' when speaking of the founding generation, whereas for later generations the constitution 'may operate more as an arranged marriage in which consent is passive' (Murphy, 1993, p.9). If we may apply this somewhat frivolous comparison to the French case it is obvious that the French, rather than passively accommodating to the routine and triteness of a long marriage, prefer to start afresh if they feel that the previous bond no longer fits their needs. The constitution is no less important for them, but their underlying idea is that it should not embody the spirit of a past venerable event which should be inscribed into the collective memory of the nation, but rather should become the historically changing incarnation of the essence of the French nation, namely its supreme power, creativity and authority to freely and independently pursue its historical mission. In other words, while the Americans find their self-assurance as a nation in the preservation of the solemn founding act as authenticated in their constitution, for the French the existence of their nation is a matter of course which is not embodied in the constitution, but in the general will of its constituent power – and this is not a sacred incident of the past, but an essential and hence eternal attribute.

Thus, in the last analysis constitutionalism involves much deeper issues than the idea of limited government, important as this undoubtedly is. At the heart of the concept of constitutionalism lies the question of how to find a way of civilising the unfathomable charisma of politics without destroying liberty. Europe was the continent where this question emerged for the first time in the history of humanity. Meanwhile, since the downfall of the bipolar world and the end of communism, the search for the right answers has become almost universal. Paradoxically, this coincides with a similarly unique step which Europe is about to make, namely the search for a constitution for a supranational political community. Will the multifaceted concept of constitutionalism as developed in the last 300 years provide us with the wisdom that is required for the solution of this new problem? Evidently this is a quite new issue which patently displays that no discussion of constitutionalism whatsoever will ever be concluded. This, then, is my provisional conclusion.

Notes

1   The present constitution establishes the Constitutional Council, which is more a council of elder statespeople and experienced politicians than of jurists. It has to check the constitutionality of organic laws *before* their enactment, whereas the compatibility of ordinary laws with the constitution *can* be scrutinised *before* their promulgation upon request of the President of the Republic, the Prime Minister of the Presidents of the two chambers of the Parliament.

References

Arendt, H. (1973), *On Revolution*, Harmondsworth: Penguin.
Bodin, J. (1962), *The Six Bookes of a Commonweale*, first published 1576, trans. R. Knolles, McRae, K.D. (ed.), Harvard University Press: Cambridge, Mass.
Bridge, J. (1995), 'The Rule of Law and the Individual in the United Kingdom and in a Federal Europe', paper presented to the conference on *Constitutional History and the Rule of Law*, Bangalore, 16–18 February.
de Bracton, H. (1968), *De Legibus et Consuetudinibus Angliae*, trans. Samuel E. Thorne, Harvard University Press: Cambridge, Mass.
Dicey, A.V. (1982), *Introduction to the Study of the Law of the Constitution*, reprint of the eighth edition of 1915, Liberty Classics: Indianapolis.
Gaus, F.F. (1994), 'Public Reason and the Rule of Law' in Shapiro, I. (ed.), *The Rule of Law*, (Nomos XXXVI), New York University Press: New York/London.
Grey, T. (1984), 'The Constitution as Scripture', *Stanford Law Review*, 37, 1–25.
Hobbes, T. (1841), *Leviathan: the Latin Version*, *Opera philosophica quae Latine scripsit omnia*, Vol. 3, J. Bohn: London.
Hobbes, T. (1991), *Leviathan*, first published 1651, Tuck, R. (ed.), Cambridge University Press: Cambridge.
Henkin, L. (1989), 'Revolutions and Constitutions', *Louisiana Law Review*, Vol. 49 , pp.1023–56.
Holmes, S. (1988), 'Precommitment and the paradox of democracy' in Elster, J. and Slagstad, R. (eds.), *Constitutionalism and Democracy*, Cambridge University Press: Cambridge/New York.
Jellinek, G. (1919), *Gesetz und Verordnung*, (v. 1887), Neudruck d. Ausg.: Tübingen.
Lacey, M.J. and Haakonssen, K. (eds.) (1992), *A Culture of Rights: The Bill of Rights in philosophy, politics, and law – 1791 and 1991*, Cambridge University Press: Cambridge.

Luhmann, N. (1974), 'Reflexive Mechanismen', *Soziologische Aufklärung*, 4, Aufl. Opladen, pp.92–112.

Luhmann, N. (1972), *Rechtssoziologie*, Rowohlt: Beinbek b. Hamburg.

Madison, J. (1961), *The Federalist Papers*, No. 51, Rossiter, C. (ed.), New American Library: New York/London.

Murphy, W.F. (1993), 'Constitutions, Constitutionalism, and Democracy' in Greenberg, D., Katz, S.N. et al. (eds.), *Constitutionalism and Democracy. Transitions in the Contemporary World*, Oxford University Press: New York/Oxford.

Paine, T. (1979), *Rights of Man*, Collins, H. (ed.), Penguin: Harmondsworth.

Rousseau, J.-J. (1968), *The Social Contract*, trans. Cranston, M. (ed.), Penguin: Harmondsworth.

Sen, A. (1994), 'Freedoms and Needs', *New Republic*, Vol. 31, January, pp.10–7.

Sieyès, E.J. (1963), *What is the Third Estate?*, first published 1789, trans. and introduced by Finer, S.E. and Blondel, M. (eds.), Pall Mall Press: London.

Taylor, C. (1992), 'Can Canada Survive the Charter?', *Alberta Law Review*, Vol. XXX, pp.427–47.

Weber, M. (1978), *Economy and Society*, Roth, G. and Wittich, C. (eds), University of Berkeley Press: Berkeley/Los Angeles/London.

Section Two
CONSTITUTIONALISM AND DEMOCRATIC POLITICS

3 Rights discourse, new social movements and new political subjects

Elizabeth Kingdom

Introduction

This chapter addresses the issue of the adequacy of rights discourse to progressive politics. Its focus is the suitedness of rights discourse to the political objectives of new social movements and to the construction of new political subjects participating in those new social movements.

In the literature of new social movements, the use of rights discourse is characterised by what, for convenience, I call the bifurcation model. From a position of shared commitment to progressive politics, activists and analysts adopt bifurcating strategies in relation to rights discourse. Briefly, either the use of rights discourse is seen as a strategy to be abandoned or as one to be deployed with new vigour. On the one hand, it is identified as a strategy which preserves the prerogative of the very legal and political structures occasioning the new social movement in question. Indeed, in reproducing the construction of political subjects as the individual bearers of rights crucial to capitalist discourse, rights discourse is seen as law's preferred discourse. On the other hand, the retention of rights discourse is defended as a strategy the established and symbolic power of which is essential to the construction of new political subjects participating in and constructed by those new social movements.

My argument in this chapter is that the identification of these strategies as mutually exclusive is an oversimplification. The bifurcation model oversimplifies the political possibilities of new social movements and it oversimplifies the political range of new political subjects. It also presents rights discourse as a discourse to be invoked in advance of political action. Accordingly, I argue that critical analysts should reject the bifurcation model. To that end, I outline an approach to the use of rights discourse which avoids that dilemma, and to support that approach I put forward a reconceptualisation of rights in terms of heuristics.

31

In the first section, 'Rights discourse – conservative trap or progressive weapon?', I exhibit some of the main arguments which have constituted the bifurcation model. A preliminary focus is American black feminists' counterattack on the Critical Legal Studies repudiation of rights discourse. The main focus is the recent renewal of comparable debates surrounding the Canadian Charter of Rights and Freedoms. In the second section, 'New social movements and new political subjects', I argue that the bifurcation model oversimplifies the analysis both of new social movements and of new political subjects. This is because neither the new social movements nor the new political subjects participating in them or constructed by them can automatically be designated politically progressive. Drawing on the work of Chantal Mouffe, I argue that there can be no *a priori* or comprehensive answer to the question of whether rights discourse should be used for the attainment of the political objectives of new social movements.

Accordingly, in the third section, 'Rights as heuristics', I propose a reconceptualisation of rights as heuristics, to the effect that the claiming of a right can be seen as the initiation of a research programme to ascertain the likely outcome of the realisation of that right, for example in the context of feminist body politics. Rights-as-heuristics is not, however, a rationalistic approach. It does not work from the presumption that the appeal to rights discourse is always the precursor of political activity. On the contrary, the calculations necessitated by rights-as-heuristics concern not only the outcomes of attempts at the implementation of rights but also the circumstances of their discovery and transformation.

Rights discourse – conservative trap or progressive weapon?

The Critical Legal Studies movement (CLS) has developed a sustained attack on the use of rights discourse for progressive politics. CLS conceptualises rights as the accepted, and preferred, discourse of the very legal and political structures – the 'establishment' structures of capitalism – that have reproduced inequality (Tushnet, 1984). CLS work and positions consonant with it have attracted vehement criticism from participants in new social movements and their sympathisers. For example, black feminists such as Patricia Williams (1990, p.45) point out that the CLS position deconstructs rights from the vantage point of those social groups who have enjoyed the protection of rights. Further, Williams avers, the CLS position priorities class politics over the politics of new social movements in a way which fails to recognise the specificity of black oppression and which neglects the motivational power of rights discourse. Her position is that for the historically disempowered, the conferring of rights is symbolic of all the aspects of their humanity which have been denied (Williams, 1990, p.47).

In recent years, these debates have been renewed in the context of the politics of the Canadian Charter of Rights and Freedoms. Judy Fudge and Harry Glasbeek (1992, p.57) have argued that whatever the benefits of specific rights, such as suspects' rights to counsel, the hegemonic power of legal and state politics has removed the radical content of rights discourse. For Fudge and Glasbeek, only class analysis provides the criterion for distinguishing those forms of contemporary resistance which will transform society and those which will leave its structures untouched. They oppose the use of rights discourse on the grounds that the presentation of rights claims is functionally compatible with dominant forms of politics. They insist that the making of political demands in terms of rights is incapable of producing social change which is other than superficial. In the particular case of new social movements with specific constituencies – women, gays and lesbians, and people of colour – using rights discourse permits the assimilation of those new social movements under the power of law and legalised politics, effectively removing the radical content of those rights demands. Like Joel Bakan and Michael Smith (1995), they remain sceptical of the capacity of rights discourse to transform contemporary social relations.

In direct opposition to Fudge and Glasbeek, Didi Herman (1994) rejects what she terms 'class instrumentalism', the dogmatic insistence that the transformation of the economic basis of society would be followed by the erosion of sexism, racism and compulsory heterosexuality. Herman (1994, p.40) therefore defends the politics of new social movements dedicated to social and cultural change and she makes a strong case for shifting the rights debate away from formal declarations of rights, conventions and charters and on to the territory of values and the deployment of power. But Herman's defence of the use of rights discourse is nuanced, and I shall return to it when I propose the reconceptualisation of rights as heuristics.

Without prejudice to that argument, however, Alan Hunt (1993, p.227) is accurate in his remark that the pro-rights and the anti-rights positions are as far apart as ever. The bifurcation model is still in position: either new social movements abandon rights discourse, in the interests of maintaining the distance from conventional power structures which is necessary to the preservation of the movements' political integrity, or new social movements deploy rights discourse and incur the risk of movements' assimilation under the very power structures resistance to which occasioned the emergence of the movements in the first place.

But I argue that to present the evaluation of rights discourse for progressive politics in terms of the bifurcation model is to oversimplify both the political possibilities of new social movements and the political range of the new political subjects participating in and constructed by them. It is to underestimate the variety of forms which social movements can take and the variety of conditions under which new political subjects may be produced. It also preserves a notion of rights discourse as a homogeneous and unitary discourse which predates political activity, as well as neglecting the variety of ways in which rights discourse can be deployed in legal and political contexts.

New social movements and new political subjects

New social movements

Not surprisingly, the literature of new social movements contains no agreed definition or analysis of them. David Plotke (1995, p.113) remarks that there have been many empirical referents for the term, and he mentions feminist movements, the gay movement, the environmental movement, some movements among racial minorities, and anti-nuclear campaigns. The problem is not with citing the examples but with providing an analytic account of their common features.

Alan Scott (1990, pp.16–8) provides one of the most succinct accounts of the defining characteristics of new social movements. He identifies three of their most prominent features. First, new social movements are primarily social, in the sense that their concern is less with citizenship and political power than with mobilisation around values and life styles. In this way, new social movements contrast with workers' movements, the suffragette movement and earlier black movements. Second, new social movements are located within civil society. They 'bypass the state' in the sense that they do not challenge the state directly but seek to defend civil society against the state's encroachment. Indeed, distance from the state is not only a condition of the success of new social movements; it is also a condition of the redefinition of the public/private spheres and of the possibility of reformation of the social groups and individuals participating in the movement in question. Third, the focus of new social movements is social and cultural change which is to be effected through the development of alternative life styles.

One reasonable inference from this account, and from many others, of new social movements is that they have in common resistance to, if not direct engagement with, dominant forms of politics as well as to prevailing cultural and social norms. That resistance suggests at least an affinity with left wing, socialist and democratic politics. Yet this analysis of new social movements can be challenged both empirically and theoretically. The empirical challenge would include a reference to Scott's account of the German ecology movement in which he brings out the conflict between left and right elements comprising that movement. Similarly, a major element in Didi Herman's (1994, pp.77–102) analysis of the struggles of Canadian lesbians and gays for equality is the new social movement broadly characterised as the New Christian Right. The theoretical challenge can be exemplified by the work of Chantal Mouffe (1988).

34

Mouffe's starting point is an attack on the class reductionism of classical Marxism, arguing that the complexity of social life is not reducible to a single economic logic. Accordingly, she argues that new social movements, such as the struggles against racism and sexism, cannot be analysed solely in terms of production. Instead, Mouffe (1988, pp.92–3) proposes, new social movements have emerged in response to the hegemonic formation which was fully installed after the Second World War. She characterises this formation in terms of the expansion of capitalist relations of production into the entire range of social life, so that everything from culture and leisure to death and sex are subordinated to the logic of commodification and to bureaucratisation. New social movements emerge as forms of resistance to the increasing homogenisation of social life and to the uniformity of mass culture imposed by the media. For Mouffe, there is no reason to suppose that new social movements will express their resistance in terms of new discourses. On the contrary, a social movement may appropriate a range of existing discourses, and it is this possibility that theorises the potential of new social movements for being hostile to socialism and anti-democratic.

Mouffe (1988, p.96) theorises the possibility of forms of popular consciousness and resistance being expressed in, or articulated to, the politics of the right with the distinction between democratic antagonisms and democratic struggles. She applies the term 'democratic antagonism' to all forms of resistance to subordination and inequality but she restricts the term 'democratic struggle' to those forms of resistance which are part of the politics of the comprehensive democratisation of social life. For example, the democratic antagonism of a newly unemployed person may take the form of a certain reaction, such as suicide or domestic violence, but democratic struggle of the unemployed will be linked to the struggles of all the oppressed. On Mouffe's analysis, the unemployed may well construct an antagonism not in terms of a critique of the domination of capitalism but in terms of an opposition to feminism, with its support for women to defend their position in the labour market, or in terms of hostility to anti-racism, with its support for black workers.

New political subjects

Mouffe's challenge to the inference that new social movements are left wing and socialist also prompts a review of the way in which the political subjects participating in new social movements are theorised. On the one hand, participants in new social movements might theorise themselves and be theorised as aspiring to the status of new political subjects in the sense of being an addition to the existing list of political subjects. For example, participants in the new social movement focusing on disability issues clearly identify themselves as campaigning for a place on the list of those political subjects protected by existing equality legislation. On the other hand, participants in new social movements might aspire to that status not in the sense of being newly subject to existing political constraints, but of being subjects in a new politics. For example, those campaigning against the transport of live calves might aspire to the status of political subjects in a form of politics which resists all forms of speciesism.

These accounts of new political subjects are easily theorised in terms of Mouffe's distinction between democratic antagonism and democratic struggle and in terms of the use of rights discourse. First, participants in new social movements may appropriate existing discourses to express their resistance. For example, they may appropriate the discourse of the political subject as the bearer of rights, the preferred discourse of legal and state institutions. To the extent that participants in new social movements such as gay and lesbian movements deploy traditional concepts of rights, Mouffe could theorise them as involved in democratic antagonism. That theorisation would derive first from the identification of traditional rights discourse as the one in which human individuals are the natural bearers of pre-social rights and, second, from the theoretical location of that discourse in the liberal ideology necessary to the operation of free markets (cf. Kingdom, 1995, pp. 4–5), an ideology hostile to the comprehensive democratisation of social life.

Further, Mouffe could argue that there is an ideological affinity between, on the one hand, that 'capitalist-friendly' concept of individuals as natural bearers of rights which are given independently of all social contingency and, on the other hand, one of the key features of new social movements identified by Scott, namely a focus on cultural change to be effected through the development of alternative life styles, an emphasis on 'identity politics'. Tamar Pitch (1995) has noted that the increased potentialities for the control and manipulation of personal identity by Western societies is matched by an enormous growth in the capacity of social actors to participate in the production of their own identity. In particular, she observes (p.79):

> The struggle of actors to appropriate control over the production of their own identity tends to express itself though an appeal to 'nature'. ... The social is constructed as repressive and manipulative of true internal nature.

Pitch clearly has reservations about this strategy, in so far as it opposes the natural to the social. Indeed, a great part of feminist literature, the literature of one new social movement, is devoted to the deconstruction of the concept of the natural, not least for its ideological support for the reproduction of atavistic concepts of gender relations. But Pitch's main concern is that the natural–social opposition risks the conversion of a new social movement into a closed sect. In Mouffe's terms, a new social movement which deploys the discourse of a natural subject as the bearer of individual rights would be more consonant with the designation of that new social movement as representing democratic antagonism than as representing democratic struggle.

But if participants in new social movements, new political subjects, are to avoid the ideological and political pitfalls of expressing their campaigns in terms of the natural human being possessed of pre-social rights, and if they resist the description of their campaigns as democratic antagonism, then they have a dual task. As well as attending to the positioning of their movement within the politics of the comprehensive democratisation of social life, they have to confront the strategic problem of devising campaign discourses other than traditional rights discourse. So far, however, the task of producing a viable alternative to that rights discourse has foiled critical analysts. No doubt it is the absence of an agreed alternative discourse that supports the bifurcation model, or at least a certain ambivalence towards the deployment of rights discourse. Mouffe's position is a striking example of this ambivalence.

Mouffe on rights

Mouffe's ambivalence over rights discourse is striking for the following reasons. Her theorisation of the difference between democratic antagonism and democratic struggle accounts for the way in which new social movements can be right wing and new political subjects can be anti-democratic. One might therefore expect Mouffe to extend her analysis to include the dismantling of the bifurcation model. In fact, Mouffe's discussion of rights retains the form of the bifurcation model, although she does not attempt to decide between the competing strategies.

On the one hand, within her characterisation of the distinction between democratic antagonism and democratic struggle, Mouffe (1988, p.100) seems to support the definition and demand of many new rights:

> Many new rights are being defined and demanded: those of women, of homosexuals, of various regional and ethnic minorities. ... In addition to these traditional social subjects [for example, industrial workers], we must recognize the existence of others and their political characters: women and the various minorities also have a right to equality and to self-determination.

Here Mouffe speaks as if the use of rights discourse were an uncontroversial political strategy.

On the other hand, Mouffe proposes that an antagonism can emerge when a collective subject (that is, a group of individuals identified in a specific way) which has been defined according to its possession of rights finds itself in a position where its rights are denied by certain practices or discourses. For example, workers may see their rights denied by the recognition of other groups' rights. Here Mouffe (1988, p.103) points to competition between rights:

> The rights of some exist because others are in a subordinate position. ... The workers now have some rights by virtue of the oppression of blacks and women; the demand to give these oppressed groups their rights must mean that some of the rights of workers must be abridged).

Further, Mouffe's (1988, p.100) theorisation of new political subjects displays a hostility to rights discourse:

> The defence of acquired rights is therefore a serious obstacle to the establishment of true equality for all.

From this position of ambivalence towards rights discourse, Mouffe (1988, p.100)hints that the pros and cons of deploying it can be settled not by opting for one strategy in preference to another but by recourse to transcending rights discourse altogether:

> A new conception of democracy also requires that we transcend a certain individualistic conception of rights and that we elaborate a central notion of *solidarity*. This can only be achieved if the rights of certain subjects are not defended to the detriment of the rights of other subjects.

Now, I have argued elsewhere that the effect of attempts to resolve political issues through the invocation of discourses which transcend prevailing social conditions is to introduce a necessary and unbridgeable gap between such discourses and the development of and engagement with questions of practical legal politics and social policy (Kingdom, 1991, p.56). Similarly, I would argue here that, despite the sophistication of her theorisation of the political diversity of new social movements and new political subjects, Mouffe's plea for a transcending ideology of solidarity leaves untouched the bifurcation model. It is effectively a reiteration of that model, and as such it preserves a very limited conception of the adequacy of rights discourse to new social movements.

In the next section, then, I outline an approach to the use of rights discourse which is not predicated on the bifurcation model. On the contrary, this approach undermines the model by collapsing the choice between two mutually exclusive strategies over rights discourse into a statement of two possible strategies for progressive politics. These two strategies are therefore to be placed within a broader range of strategic calculations, a range of calculations introduced by the notion of rights as heuristics.

Rights as heuristics

To resume discussion of Herman's position, her emphasis on the political importance of new social movements is accompanied by her defence of the use of rights discourse. But she does not argue for the simple reassertion of individual or human rights. In her detailed analysis of the struggles for lesbian and gay equality in Canada, Herman (1994, p.9) explicitly seeks to avoid the polarity of the rights debate:

> [R]ights are neither good nor bad. Instead, rights claims and rhetoric play unpredictable and contradictory roles in social struggle; and their effects are complex and changing.

It is important to guard against a misinterpretation of Herman's position here. Despite the above characterisation of the complex role of rights, Herman's resistance to the position of Fudge and Glasbeek, and her clear defence of the use of rights discourse, might appear to preserve a particular notion of rights discourse. This is a conception of rights discourse the suitability of which to particular campaigns comprises, if not the first calculation of a campaign, then at least an early one. To caricature such a view, one would picture campaigners settling down early on in their activities to a brainstorming session, raiding the rights discourse treasury for usable moral positions and slogans to match.

In fact, Herman (1994, p.76) is careful to argue that the rights debate is not usefully conducted in the abstract and that notions of rights themselves shift. Her analysis of rights discourse here points to the necessity of specific analyses of the vicissitudes of rights discourse in particular political and legal contexts (cf. Lepervanche, 1989) and the complexities of transition from social movement to interest group (cf. Costain, 1982).

To capture this emphasis on the uncertainties of rights discourse and the importance of context-specific evaluations of its use, I propose this reconceptualisation of rights: rights as heuristics. Following the use of the term 'heuristic' in epistemology as a principle for the direction of the production of knowledge, a heuristic device is one which serves to focus attention on a specific area of research. In the context of legal politics and in the context of new social movements, then, to conceptualise rights as heuristics is a mechanism for directing attention to a specific area of practical politics. I would stress immediately that the rights-as-heuristics approach is not predicated on the logical, temporal or political priority of rights discourse over political activity. On the contrary, as I shall argue, rights-as-heuristics can accommodate the devising and the discovery of rights.

Four illustrations now follow of rights-as-heuristics. The first three happen to fall within the politics of the new social movement of feminism, but there is no reason why similar examples could not be given in the context of, for example, environmentalist politics.

In the first instance, the declaration of women's rights in a particular sphere of politics is a mechanism for bringing to prominence a feminist interest in that political context and for identifying the research necessary to formulating appropriate policies. In the context of feminist body politics, for example, the claim of a woman's right to bodily integrity would be understood as the mechanism around which research could be conducted into legal and medical practices regarding the withholding of consent to Caesarian sections, into the beneficial and disadvantageous effects of medicalising women's decisions in the area of reproductive technology (cf. Sheldon, 1995), and into the merits of different approaches from medicalisation in other jurisdictions (cf. Millns, 1995). In this way, the claim of a right to bodily integrity ceases to be a moral imperative and becomes a feature of a research programme. In this respect, feminists in the UK will sensibly peruse descriptions of strategies adopted by feminists in other jurisdictions and evaluate their success or defeat (cf. Kingdom, 1995, pp.17–8).

A key item in such a research programme would be the calculation of the adequacy of rights discourse for feminist campaigns for empowerment and autonomy. I have argued elsewhere that there can be no *a priori* answer to that question in the area of feminist body politics (Kingdom, 1991). Sometimes the appeal to rights, such as a woman's right to choose, can have deleterious effects, such as 'attracting' the competing rights of a foetus or of a man (Kingdom, 1991, pp.46–62). Sometimes prevailing legal politics is ineluctably framed in terms of rights discourse, such as international declarations of rights, and it would be politically naive to suppose that feminist interventions in such a sphere could be successful if they too were not expressed in terms of rights (Kingdom, 1995, pp.10–1). It follows from these observations that the decision to adopt or reject rights discourse cannot be made according to a single rule; the decision has to be context-specific, paying attention to foreseeable consequences, past experiences, and shifting debates (cf. Bala, 1994).

A second illustration of how rights-as-heuristics can assist in the formulation of policy is provided by the collection of papers on *Women, Equal Opportunities and Welfare in the European Community* (O'Brien et al., 1990). The starting point is a catalogue of the various formal declarations of rights emanating from the European Union. These are mostly directives, and they are accompanied by a description of the mechanisms established for their implementation. But the contributors then convert the formal declarations of rights into research programmes, both theoretical and policy orientated. Of particular importance is the contribution by Janet Finch. She points to feminists' disillusion with the implementation to date of women's rights and she locates that disillusion in the opposition between two models for the construction of women's welfare rights (Finch, 1990, pp.1–4). On the one hand, the European Community predicates women's welfare rights on rights linked to participation in the paid labour market, and accordingly limits women's access to benefits such as social insurance. Finch, however, argues for a model of women's rights as constructed on the basis of citizenship, on the grounds that this model recognises women's social role as providers of welfare services and basic health care support. The juxtaposition of these two models, I suggest, is an illustration of how rights-as-heuristics demands attention both to the empirical analysis of practical machinery of European legislation and to the theoretical investigation of ideologies and conventions shaping policies and practices.

In this example, rights-as-heuristics again dismantles the notion of rights discourse as prior to political activity and converts it into the initiation of a research programme which may be undertaken at any stage in a political campaign and at any point in the practices of a new social movement. In the example under consideration, the research programme is not predicated on the assumption that feminists are confronted with a straightforward choice between using or not using rights discourse. That is to say, these feminists are not confronted with the bifurcation model. Rather, they are confronted with the problem of trying to displace one form of rights discourse with another.

The third example of rights-as-heuristics is also instructive in this respect. Katherine Culliton (1993) proposes the redefinition of women's right to life and their right to physical integrity to include the interpretation of domestic violence and rape as torture, thereby bringing these offences under the sway of considerable portions of international law. Culliton's work demonstrates clearly the limitation of assuming that rights discourse is a pre-political discourse which can in some way be applied to the campaigns of new social movements, prior to their political activity. For Culliton does not reject or support rights discourse, nor does she see her project as an ideological dilemma over the priority of class analysis. In this respect, she is not constrained by the parameters of the bifurcation model. Her investigation reviews the potential of a strategy calculated to address what feminists have seen as a known legal–political inattention to their concerns. Culliton's proposal clearly undermines the bifurcation model and alerts readers' attention to the feasibility of reviewing, creating, or perhaps finding, a right.

In this respect, Geoffrey Kennett's work provides an instructive fourth example of rights-as-heuristics. He observes that the framers of the Australian Constitution had little interest in the inclusion of individual rights in the Constitution, both because they were suspicious of how the generality of constitutional rights discourse could lead to unintended consequences and because they had confidence in Parliament as the protector of rights. Kennett (1994, p.581) notes, however that in recent years, judges have started to *find* rights in the Constitution:

[I]ndividual rights have been found lurking in unlikely provisions of the Constitution. Recently, in *Nationwide News Pty Ltd v. Wills* and *Australian Capital Television Pty Ltd v. Commonwealth*, the Court found a freedom of political communication inherent in the basic structure of the Constitution.

Kennett's analysis is an antidote to the notion that the use of rights discourse is always the precursor of legal politics and it points to the way in which scrutiny of legal discourse can yield surprising examples of how rights discourse can operate and become a new feature of legal politics. Like Culliton's, Kennett's project is not predicated on the dilemma of using or not using rights discourse. Kennett's work is predicated on what might be called an intrigue. The intrigue is the friction between his expectation that rights discourse would have featured in the debates preceding the passing of the Constitution and his reading of the aftermath of the Constitution. Kennett's analysis does not so much address the adequacy of rights discourse to legal politics as represent a research directive, an alertness to appearances of rights discourse which constitute a shift in the terms of a particular debate, a shift which may itself be exploitable for specific legal politics. In that way, Kennett's work is in keeping with the main argument of this chapter.

Conclusion

I have argued that the adequacy of rights discourse to new social movements should not be discussed in terms of the bifurcation model. This is partly because new social movements and the new political subjects participating in them cannot be theorised as automatically progressive, socialist or democratic. It is also because the use of rights discourse itself can be seen neither as a discourse which always precedes legal and political activity, nor as a discourse which has a single legal and political career. Accordingly, I have argued that critical analysts should resist the pressure to make *a priori* judgments on the efficacy of rights discourse for advancing progressive politics.

To that end, I have proposed a conceptualisation of rights in terms of heuristics, a mechanism for progressive politics in terms of research programmes. Such research programmes may involve identifying different models of rights within a certain legal–political context and pressing for the abandonment of one model in favour of another. They may involve the reconceptualisation of a right so as to bring it within the range of promising legislation. Rights-as-heuristics also involves a general vigilance for the unexpected vicissitudes of rights discourse. Curiously, the opening paragraph of this chapter could itself be a target of rights-as-heuristics. The phrase 'adequacy of rights discourse to progressive politics' could be taken to imply the epistemological or political priority of rights discourse over political activity. But the burden of this chapter is that rights-as-heuristics makes no *a priori* judgment about the adequacy – or inadequacy – of rights discourse to progressive politics.

References

Bakan, J.C. and Smith, M. (1995), 'According to rights: the Charlottestown accord and rights politics', *Social and Legal Studies*, Vol. 4, No. 4, pp.367–90.

Bala, N. (1994), 'The Evolving Canadian definition of the family: towards a pluralistic and functional approach', *International Journal of Law and the Family*, Vol. 8, pp.293–318.

Costain, A.E. (1982), 'Representing women: the transition from social movement to interest group' in Boneparth, E. (ed.), *Women, Power and Policy*, Pergamon: Oxford.

Culliton, K. (1993), 'Finding a mechanism to enforce women's right to state protection from domestic violence in the Americas', *Harvard International Law Journal*, Vol. 34, No. 2, pp.507–61.

Finch, J. (1990), 'Women, equal opportunities and welfare in the European Community: some questions and issues', Guest Editorial in O'Brien, M., Hantras, L. and Mangen, S. (eds.), *Women, Equal Opportunities and Welfare*, The Cross-National Research Group: Aston University.

Fudge, J. and Glasbeek, H. (1992), 'The Politics of rights: politics with little class', *Social and Legal Studies*, Vol. 1, No. 1, pp.45–70.

Herman, D. (1994), *Rights of Passage: Struggles for Lesbian and Gay Legal equality*, University of Toronto Press: London.

Hunt, A. (1993), 'Rights and social movements: counterhegemonic strategies' in *Explorations in Law and Society*, Routledge: London.

Kennett, G. (1994), 'Individual rights, the High Court and the Constitution', *Melbourne University Law Review*, Vol. 19, No. 3, pp.581–614.

Kingdom, E. (1991), *What's Wrong with Rights?: Problems for Feminist Politics of Law*, Edinburgh University Press: Edinburgh.

Kingdom, E. (1995), 'Body politics and rights' in Bridgeman, J. and Millns, S. (eds.), *Law and Body Politics: Regulating the Female Body*, Dartmouth: Aldershot.

Lepervanche, M. de (1989), 'Women, nation and the state in Australia' in Yuval-Davis, N. and Anthias, F. (eds.), *Woman-Nation-State*, Macmillan: London.

Millns, S. (1995), 'Making social judgments that go beyond the purely medical: the reproductive revolution and access to fertility treatment' in Bridgeman and Millns (eds.), op. cit.

Mouffe, C. (1988), 'Hegemony and new political subjects: toward a new concept of democracy' in Nelson, C. and Grossberg, L. (eds.), *Marxism and the Interpretation of Culture*, University of Illinois Press: Urbana and Chicago.

O'Brien, M., Hantras, L. and Mangen, S. (eds.), *Women, Equal Opportunities and Welfare*, The Cross-National Research Group: Aston University.

Pitch, T. (1995), *Limited Responsibilities: Social Movements and Criminal Justice*, trans. John Lea, Routledge: London.

Plotke, D. (1995), 'What's so new about new social movements?' in Lyman, S.M. (ed.), *Social Movements: Critiques, Concepts, Case-studies*, Macmillan: London.

Scott, A. (1990), *Ideology and the New Social Movements*, Unwin Hyman: London.

Sheldon, S. (1995), 'The law of abortion and the politics of medicalisation' in Bridgeman, J. and Millns, S. (eds.), *Law and Body Politics*, Dartmouth: Aldershot.

Tushnet, M. (1984), 'An Essay on rights', *Texas Law Review*, Vol. 62, pp.1363–97.

Williams, P. (1990), *The Alchemy of Race and Rights*, Virago: London.

4 Righting wrongs: the normality of constitutional politics

Vivien Hart

Rights claims and constitutional politics have taken something of a beating of late. Their current disfavour is a new twist in a long Anglo-American comparative history, stretching from Bryce (1888) and Dicey (1905) to Ryan (1991) and Beer (1993). The affirmative experience of the American civil rights movement and the commitment of a movement of American women to an Equal Rights Amendment to the Constitution were formative episodes for the modern politics of rights, generating enthusiasm and then reaction. Traditional British scepticism has been contested but not defeated by growing, organised demands for constitutional reform including a Bill of Rights, and by discovery of the political uses of rights in European Union treaties (Ryan, 1991; Hart, 1996).

Rights are prominent on the British and American political agenda of the 1990s, at a moment of questioning rather than the optimism of the civil rights era. An important theoretical debate, driven particularly by the concerns of socialist, feminist and critical legal theorists, has, as Elizabeth Kingdom (1991) has pointed out, polarised into irreconcilable alternatives. Either rights are tools of oppressive capitalism, patriarchy or legal process or rights are opportunities for the oppressed to make invigorating and morally powerful claims on the state. The debate is important, but the warning of a labour activist, frustrated by the search for theoretical perfection, remains timely. Pauline Newman, of the ILGWU, testified to a New York State commission after a sweatshop fire in 1911 in which 146 women died. While experts talked about what might be effective, efficient, desirable and constitutional, she snapped, 'in the meantime, the girls are absolutely starved' (quoted in Hart, 1994, p.xii).

Kingdom's solution to the potential paralysis induced by profound disagreement is to propose in this volume a model of 'rights as heuristics', framing a set of questions about strategy and outcome for social movements. Her model imposes a sense of context and contingency on discussions of constitutionalism and rights politics. Rights are, as she earlier reminded us, a fact of national and international political systems in the late 20th century which cannot be wished away by those who mistrust their promises (Kingdom, 1991, p.4). There may be circumstances in which it is constructive as well as necessary to adopt the language of rights in formulating claims and strategies. Social movements must understand whether and in what circumstances constitutional promises are a resource. Bruce Ackerman (1991) has proposed that social movements in the United States do understand exactly this. Ackerman (1991, p.6) offers another dichotomy, between 'normal' and 'constitutional' politics. In the dualist American democracy, 'normal lawmaking' is the daily, continuous process of politics and policymaking. 'Constitutional politics' occurs rarely, under conditions of extreme discontent and the exceptional mobilisation of private citizens (who are normally absent, for sundry bad and good reasons, from political activity) into social movements. The goal of such movements is 'higher lawmaking', the redress of broken constitutional promises to the People or the transformation of the constitutional settlement itself. A successful movement will 'ultimately gain the constitutional authority to make new law in the name of We the People of the United States' (Ackerman, 1991, p.57).

Amidst such questioning about the nature and role of constitutionalism, while Americans have second thoughts about the politics of rights and the British debate whether formal rights would be a positive innovation, the constitutional practice is changing. The American Supreme Court shows signs of unravelling rights once thought secure. In Britain, a form of constitutional politics analogous to the American experience is developing. Constitutional theory has rarely been debated wholly in the abstract. Discussion of the inherent nature of rights need not be, but frequently is, driven by practice and theories of rights have blossomed and faded with the fortunes of rights politics. Both models, that of rights as heuristics, rights as instrumental, contingent, political devices and that of the Constitution as an intermittent and fundamental site of contest, directly suggest an agenda of empirical research into whether such propositions in general hold, whether generalisations about specific contingencies are possible and to what extent any conclusions may be helpful to the theory and practice of social movements.

The modern history of rights politics in America, outlined in my next section, has been formative in generating such an agenda. Americans have not necessarily found the proper questions or correct answers. But rights politics in the United States attracted the attention of the world in the 1950s, when international instruments like the European Convention on Human Rights were in their infancy. Even for the United States, a politics of rights was a new development. The complexity and contingency of rights is not just a self-contained issue of their effectiveness. Maybe rights will be a permanent feature of politics in the future: they have not been in the past, even where a Bill of Rights has existed. In earlier decades, social movements in the United States searched the Constitution for other sources of authority for their claims, practising a broader programme of 'constitutional heuristics'. Bruce Ackerman's (1991, p.41) account, for example, identifies three decisive episodes of constitutional politics, 'jurisgenerative' moments all predating the era of rights politics: the Founding and the constitutional settlement of 1787; Reconstruction and the Thirteenth, Fourteenth and Fifteenth Amendments; and the political and legal transformation of constitutional law during the New Deal.

To explore these possibilities, the main section of this chapter outlines the history of a single policy, the minimum wage, in the United States. The Constitution was not the only factor which shaped the development of minimum wage policy. But its importance, and the dynamics of the relationship, are clarified by comparison with the parallel policy history in Britain, without a framework of codified constitutional standards. A single example only begins to establish the contingencies of constitutional politics, of rights politics, and of the contextual circumstances which influence both. It does demonstrate the historical record as a resource for latter day practitioners; indeed, though Pauline Newman might be surprised to learn it, 'rights as heuristics', as a sub genre of 'constitutions as heuristics', is something that she and her friends were doing all along.

American rights

The golden era of rights politics was surely that of the civil rights movement and the Warren Court, in the 1950s and 1960s. The litigation strategy of the NAACP since the 1920s had been to build precedents against segregation, culminating in 1954 with the overthrow of the 'separate but equal' justification (Tushnet, 1987). African-Americans enlarged both the vision of equality and the strategy, taking rights rhetoric from the courts to the streets, the lunch counters and the voting booths (Graham, 1990). Their discourse was soon shared by women, as the Equal Rights Amendment was launched for ratification in 1972 (Mansbridge, 1986). Other economically, physically and socially disadvantaged groups added their voices to a debate with great resonance in American political culture (Minow, 1990).

The framework for these claims was one of individual, civil, equal rights, relying principally on the Fourteenth Amendment promise of 'the equal protection of the laws'. Where civil rights began to shade into what Europeans would call collective social rights, the Supreme Court declined to apply to welfare recipients the standard of strict scrutiny granted to race classifications or the rights of the Equal Protection Clause (Davis, 1993). American commentators, writing within this tradition of civil, negative rights, argued that social, positive rights could not be constitutionalised, were not justiciable and were a legislative responsibility under the separation of powers (Currie, 1993). Already, major questions were on the agenda: fundamental questions of what is a right, whether social as well as civil, pertaining to groups as well as individuals; practical questions of whether rights must be limited to justiciable issues; political questions in the suspicion sown by the exclusion of welfare claimants from rights politics, that rights primarily benefit the privileged.

Questions of the symbolism, security and exercise of rights arose with the failure to ratify the Equal Rights Amendment. Doubt was reinforced by a decade of attack on abortion rights, which were undermined by both political and legal developments. In particular, the Supreme Court's conclusion that the Constitution might endow citizens with rights but the state incurred no obligation to ensure the means to exercise them, appeared to create a category of 'privately purchased public rights' beyond the reach of many citizens (Williams, 1991, p.35). Feminist arguments about the limitations of rights became more than a realistic rebalancing of theory, however, as, spurred by disillusion, essentialist counter-claims about both gender and rights were made.

The individualism of rights in the American Constitution, it was proposed, belied the connected nature of women's lives, which are lived in a web of relationships with other women, men and children (West, 1988). This could be an essentialist argument about biological difference (as well as an essentialist argument about rights as individual attributes). In some hands it was derived from the physical fact of connection in pregnancy. Often, gender appeared as a socially constructed difference, manifest in women's moral reasoning and behaviour (Gilligan, 1982, Ch. 5). The reaffirmation of women's difference in any form revived a longstanding debate. Could legal equality, here framed as equal rights, reconstruct gendered roles in family and childcare or correct the structural inequality of the labour market and other social institutions? Were rights campaigns simply contradictory to women's interests, changed by women's participation, or could they be reconceived in feminist or other form?

The feminist debate was one strand of a general reevaluation. Labour historians saw the diminution by successive judicial rulings of the hard won union right to organise as indicative of the inevitable failure of individual rights to benefit collective organisations (Klare, 1977–78). Both trade unionists and women, stung by the gap between high hopes and disappointing outcomes, identified individualism as an inherent flaw in rights politics. Mary Ann Glendon (1991) found the individualism of rights both more comprehensively destructive of the political process in America and also potentially more correctable. Applying adjectives like 'strident', 'stark' and 'simple', she deplored the way that all political claims seemed to have become reducible to rights claims. Adversarial and self-interested rights claims had driven 'the moral, the long-term, and the social implications' from the political arena (Glendon, 1991, p.171). Women and unionists sought a different kind of right, responsive to their collectivities. Glendon sought a refinement, a reining in of the 'rights foundationalists' who believed that rights claims trumped all other considerations (Ackerman, 1991, pp.13, 23). In her ideal polity, self-restrained individual rights claims would take their proper, modest, place in a communitarian polity.

The archetypal constitutional campaign, the African-American civil rights movement, has also seen a backlash in the form of repudiation of the policy of affirmative action. In this instance, however, the intention is to restore individualism. Affirmative action programmes were designed to bring equal protection to a group historically disadvantaged by discrimination. Lately, even former beneficiaries have disavowed the principle and the Supreme Court has whittled away at the constitutional foundations. In its latest term, the Court has ruled that strict scrutiny of racial classifications is to ensure that 'the personal right to equal protection has not been infringed' by 'governmental action based on race' (*Adarand v. Pena*, 1995); that programmes to eliminate school segregation should be judged by their 'demonstration of good faith' to act 'to the extent practicable' (*Missouri v. Jenkins*, 1995); and that electoral redistricting plans in which race is the 'overriding and predominant force' improperly apply 'the very stereotypical assumptions the Equal Protection Clause forbids' (*Miller v. Johnson*, 1995).

Rights and social change

Problems on the agenda thus range from the status of individual, group, civil and social rights, to the vulnerability of rights to judicial opinion, to dependence on lawyers, the necessity of judicial review, the reinforcement of privilege, divisiveness and simplification of complex moral and social questions. Given such doubts, it might well be asked whether rights are worth pursuing. There are two schools of thought on this issue too, one denying, the other defending the transformative power of rights.

The extent to which school segregation survives in America, 40 years after the *Brown* decision, is frequently cited against the effectiveness of rights. Unenforceability is added to the indictment. 'To ask [courts] to produce significant social reform ... is to cloud our vision with a naive and romantic belief in the triumph of rights over politics', Gerald Rosenberg (1991, p.343) has concluded. Rosenberg's view of rights as legal instruments is reminiscent of what Stuart Scheingold (1974, p.5) called the myth of rights; 'a direct linking of litigation, rights, and remedies with social change'. An early advocate of contingency, Scheingold (1974, p.6) viewed rights 'on the one hand, as authoritatively articulated goals of public policy and, on the other, as political resources of unknown value in the hand of those who want to alter the course of public policy'. Power, opposition and conflict enter an equation in which a right is one resource, of uncertain worth depending upon 'the circumstances and on the manner in which it is employed'.

Rights will be most valued, Richard Cortner (1968, p.287) suggested, where other political opportunities are lacking. People make constitutional claims 'usually because they are temporarily, or even permanently, disadvantaged in terms of their abilities to attain successfully their goals in the electoral process, within the elected political institutions or in the bureaucracy'. Unlike Rosenberg, Cortner evaluated access as well as results, recognising that access may be important in itself. Participation can be cooptative; it can also open dialogue and legitimate conflict resolution. A right contributes a language for the articulation of claims and standing as a rights holder within the political process; no small contribution to opening the public arena to citizens with few other political resources.

Patricia Williams (1991, p.152) goes far to explain why the two sides often seem to be talking past each other in this debate. She too believes that rights matter: 'that rights are disutile, even harmful, trivializes this aspect of black experience specifically, as well as that of any person or group whose vulnerability has been truly protected by rights'. She adds a second transformative possibility. There is the important goal of social transformation. But rights may also effect a personal transformation. Affirmative action is programmatic but also 'affirmative action is an affirmation' (Williams, 1991, p.121). At least in American political culture, centred upon the constitutional text, there is a powerful argument that the symbolism of rights is not an empty gesture. For 'the historically disempowered, the conferring of rights is symbolic of all the denied aspects of their humanity' (Williams, 1991, p.153).

Rights, the contingency argument suggests, *may* be an inspiration, a point of access and an instrument of change. But when are they so? In the golden age of rights politics, Americans 'found' rights even beyond those specified. A right to privacy located in the penumbra of the Bill of Rights is the classic example (Garrow, 1994). For decades before, the equality right of the Equal Protection Clause had been a dead letter and social movements had looked to other clauses and other penumbra (the Commerce Clause, the implied police power) for authority for their claims to a better society. Rights politics themselves, as well as the advantages and disadvantages they incur, are historically contingent. The case study of minimum wage policy which follows sets the politics of rights in the broader context of constitutional politics.

Minimum wage policy and comparative constitutionalism

A statutory minimum wage was introduced for some low paid workers in Britain in 1909 and copied by American reformers. In 1912 they won their first state law in Massachusetts. Both were sponsored by women and men reformers who were transatlantic friends and colleagues. Both addressed the same problem of sweated labour, which existed in similar dimensions and with a similar two thirds female work force. Yet the transfer of the policy from the interventionist social programme of the British Liberal government to a United States in thrall to the *laissèz faire* principle was in itself surprising. The subsequent history of the minimum wage further upsets the conventional wisdom of transatlantic differences in social policy, of British collectivism versus American individualism and the classic distinction between the supposed rigidity of a written, and flexibility of an unwritten, constitution.

For 70 years, the policy in Britain was stagnant, invisible and ineffective. After 1979, the Conservative government set out to abolish the minimum wage and in 1993 did so. In the United States the trajectory more resembled a roller-coaster. Between 1912 and 1923, the number of laws climbed to 15, plus the District of Columbia, and protected women rather than low paid workers. In 1923, rejection by the Supreme Court plunged America into a period with no enforceable policy. In an upturn in 1938, a minimum wage was legislated by the federal government, reconceived as a single flat rate figure and applied to wage labour in interstate commerce. The exclusions which this quasi-universal language concealed were gradually chipped away. As Britain moved towards abolition, America achieved near universal coverage.

In the book from which this example is taken, I have argued that the United States Constitution is the prime factor accounting for the difference between early closure of British debate over who should benefit and the intellectual leaps and bounds of the American history (Hart, 1994). This history is an education in both the enabling and disabling potential of constitutional politics, in the dialectical relationship between law and politics and in the situational and textual contingencies which arise. Constitutional, rather than rights, politics, because for several decades constitutionality hinged on the implied doctrine of the police power, on interpretation of due process and the Commerce Clause and on the definition of federalism. Alexander Hamilton's (1961, p.440) famous phrase denying the need for a separate Bill of Rights, can be simply adjusted to fit the case. In its influence on the politics of the minimum wage, the entire American Constitution indeed operated 'itself, in every rational sense, and to every useful purpose, [in the same way as] a BILL OF RIGHTS'.

The police power

American minimum wage policy is neatly periodised by landmark Supreme Court decisions: in 1908, *Muller v. Oregon* created a precedent for protective legislation for women, opening the way for gendered legislation; in 1923, in *Adkins v. Children's Hospital*, minimum wage policy was rejected and went into abeyance; in close succession in 1937 and 1941 state laws for women were reinstated (*West Coast Hotel v. Parrish*) and a new federal formula was approved (*US v. Darby*). The periodisation is correct, but the primacy implied for Supreme Court decisions is not. On closer inspection, the Court appears neither as the autonomous actor of some models of judicial policy making, erupting periodically to make or change the rules nor as a reliable agent of capitalism or patriarchy. Instead, the Court has been one participant in a social and political dialogue. Cases have been pivotal rather than declaratory, influenced by developments in politics as well as law in the preceding period, formative but not determinative of the law and politics of the period after.

The limitations imposed by the text and its interpretation are at first sight more visible than the opportunities of constitutional politics. But text and interpretations have proved amply ambiguous, riddled with loopholes and offering more than one route to the desired end. While the first response to a hostile Court decision was despair or anger, the second would always be a creative search for new legally *and* politically acceptable ways forward. Because of these characteristics of constraint, ambiguity and opportunity, social movements and the policy process in America's constitutional culture have been imbued with a habit of asking in advance as well as in reaction, both what is constitutionally difficult or impossible and how to preempt and shape the constitutional terrain to maximise success.

The conceptual, constitutional, debate on the minimum wage began long before its day in court. In 1908, when Florence Kelley (leader of the National Consumers' League and the campaign) returned from Europe with news of the British proposal, she practised constitutional heuristics as well as skilful tactical politics. The constitutional terrain looked as inhospitable as the political will to involve government in regulating wages. There were no precedents for federal legislation, there had been no prior consideration of the constitutionality of wage regulation and the closest parallels – hours, health and safety laws – had only occasionally been upheld, when health was directly at stake. Reformers were still absorbing the implications of the 1905 *Lochner v. New York* decision, which gave its name to an era of Supreme Court assertion of its own narrow view of the scope of social policy. The priority given to market forces and freedom of contract dashed the hopes of reformers that legislation could mitigate the worst exploitation and the immense social problems of the new industrial world. Only one qualification to the new doctrine that judges knew better than legislatures and would apply their dogma to the ends as well as the means chosen by elected bodies had been admitted, when a ten hour day law for women was upheld in *Muller v. Oregon* in 1908, opening a door for gendered legislation at the state level.

Constitutionally, therefore, a campaign on the British model faced a situation which was difficult in requiring multiple state campaigns, risky in the unknown status of wage regulation, near impossible as far as legislating for the 'low paid workers' of the British legislation went, but *perhaps* more receptive to a case for the female two thirds of sweated labour, *if* any wage law were to be allowed. Minimum wagers (a contemporary label) were all armchair lawyers. They viewed the Constitution as a fact of political life, a challenge, a set of choices, but never an insuperable obstacle. And the political momentum outweighed the legal hurdles.

The campaign chose its ground: minimum wage policy would find authority under the implied police power of the state to protect health, welfare and morals. Minimum wagers thus rejected advice that wage regulation was constitutionally unwinnable. They accepted the federal division of powers, and campaigned state by state. And to limit the constitutional battleground they tailored draft statutes to procedural due process standards, specifying every operational detail. All these choices were constrained by both political and legal environments. And at this time rights held no promise. Neither the rights claims of women for equal civil status nor the Equal Protection Clause had been applied to social policy, where rights meant only an equal right to individual freedom from state interference in the market.

The opening given by the *Muller* decision was for gendered legislation. To justify this, the Supreme Court laid out a comprehensive statement of gender difference. Women lacked the vote; but they also lacked the experience, resources, skills and social and psychological traits necessary to defend themselves in the labour market. It seemed challenge enough to minimum wagers to win constitutional authorisation of wage regulation for anyone. But in using the *Muller* opening, the abandonment of needy men and the implied denigration of women as 'wards of the state' were dilemmas: 'In England ... the well-being of men as well as women is held to be vital to the state', one campaigner regretted. But England was not, 'as we are', bound by constitutional limitations (quoted in Hart, 1994, p.87). The focus on gender disguised the economic dynamics of sweating and isolated or even opposed women's interests and men's. Emphasis on the effect of low wages on health drew attention to symptoms rather than causes. Campaigners justified a 'half-loaf' strategy to themselves and the courts with the reasoning that women were not inherently weaker than men but structurally disadvantaged. They argued that gender difference did not imply inequality. And that getting the camel's nose of wage regulation by any means under the constitutional tent would open the way for full coverage later.

Their British counterparts revelled in a culture of 'practical empiricism' where minimum wage legislation could pass 'in advance of other nations, before we began to look for the doctrines which underlay our action, and long before we possessed the knowledge on which it was said to be based' (quoted in Hart, 1994, p.177). A law for low paid workers matched the composition of sweated labour and need not be consistent with other policies. Basic procedural details could be delegated to Trade Boards. The advantage seems all to lie with Britain's freedom from a constitutional regime. The problems created by the British failure to resolve confusion about the relation of the policy to gender in the labour market and by the delegation of basic decisions on scope and value (unacceptable evasions in American constitutional practice) were more easily seen with hindsight.

The police power era is not, however, solely a negative for constitutional politics. Wrestling with issues of constitutionality brought questions of classification, procedure and value into the open, in a debate with no equivalent in Britain. To justify singling out women, for example, necessitated the conversion into constitutional terms of social and biological theories of gender roles, structural analyses of the labour market and labour organisation, political analyses of women's civil, pre-suffrage status, and economic arguments for modification of the sacred free market. Problematic, indeed, but in the long run such discursive necessities gave the policy a momentum and logic unmatched in Britain. Likewise, to satisfy procedural due process criteria meant specifying rules, which Parliament had delegated. The American application of even a meagre living wage standard by committed administrators seemed more open to challenge, less vulnerable to power (Hart, 1992). Transparency in debate and implementation were not negligible benefits.

The police power strategy also gave new dimensions to Cortner's concept of 'access'. Women without the vote were formally excluded from politics. Within politics, they were disadvantaged by gendered traditions of the public sphere as male, by the male culture of political activity and by primary government functions of public order, foreign policy and macro-economics which were culturally defined as male. The police power concern for health, welfare and morals embraced precisely women's traditional 'private' sphere. In industrial and urban America, these concerns had overflowed the boundaries of the home but not yet infiltrated the boundaries of the state. Under the aegis of the police power, women could enter political institutions as experts; could ask for state attention to their own concerns and in their own right; and could expand the public domain to include women's social responsibilities.

From Commerce Clause to rights

In this pervasive constitutional culture, it is not surprising that Florence Kelley began her reform career in the 1880s by qualifying as a lawyer. In 1920, she still regarded the 16 statutes on the books as 'drafts', until they should receive 'an original affirmative decision by the United States Supreme Court' (quoted in Hart, 1994, p.108). When that decision came in 1923, 15 years of anticipation proved in vain. The Supreme Court in *Adkins v. Children's Hospital of Washington, D.C.* rejected both the gender strategy and the entire rationale for regulating wages. Minimum wagers first despaired. Kelley denounced 'the inalienable constitutional right ... to starve' and called for women on the Court (quoted in Hart, 1994, p.132). The District of Columbia Minimum Wage Board, subject of the test case, shut down within days. But the campaign rallied and took the constitutional dialectic forward again.

The hurdle was higher following the *Adkins* ruling that women with suffrage needed no protection and that wage setting by these procedures was 'a naked, arbitrary exercise of power' violating due process (quoted in Hart, 1994, p.138). However, a judicial afterthought that a wage with 'fair' relation to labour value might pass muster started one new trail. A second developed in the 1930s, when all of the economy began to resemble the sweated sector, industrial unions with statist sympathies grew, New Deal programmes addressed a national economy and minimum wagers staffed the administration. Interest turned to the Commerce Clause, the congressional power to regulate commerce among the several states, and the debate became technical as administration insiders not only rewrote minimum wage policy but deliberately set out to change the prevailing judicial interpretation of the Constitution. 'The due process clauses ought to go', declared Felix Frankfurter in 1924 (quoted in Hart, 1994, p.136). The key concept of due process was not a powerful political rallying cry. Nor, compared to the police power, was it as comprehensible, nor a means of access as validating to reform activity. When *Adkins* obliterated the police power rationale, the ramifications spread beyond the collapse of policy to the leadership and tactics of the campaign.

Events in the 1930s gave ammunition to those distrustful of the judicial role. Fair wage strategists agreed again that to challenge on gender as well as due process was still one battle too far. An attempt to meet due process objections with an ingenious statute incorporating a living wage, a health wage, a fair labour value wage and an oppressive wage was rejected by the Supreme Court on a technicality (in *Morehead v. New York*, 1936). But in 1937 the minimum wage campaigners were astonished when the Court reversed *Adkins*, reinstating state laws for women. The case of *West Coast Hotel Co. v. Parrish* which achieved this unexpected turn of events was a key part of the 'switch in time' which announced the 'jurisgenerative' transformation of constitutional law during the New Deal (Ackerman, 1991, pp.49–50). The Supreme Court signalled a step back from confrontation with legislatures over interpretive control of the Constitution. Turning away from *Lochner*, the Court admitted a new respect for legislative determination of whether and how to regulate the economy and ameliorate poverty. For minimum wagers, it validated the abandoned police power strategy of thirty years before. The files of the District of Columbia Board were unboxed and within weeks it was back in business in the same room in the District Building as 14 years before. But the campaign had moved on and this was taken as encouragement to continue its new federal direction rather than to rest on its new laurel. The 1938 federal Fair Labor Standards Act (FLSA), claiming Commerce Clause authorisation, soon achieved the elusive unconditionally affirmative ruling. Politics and law again intersected, for by the time the case of *US v. Darby* was decided in 1941 both Felix Frankfurter, the brain behind the legislation and Hugo Black, its sponsor in the Senate, were on the Court and the New Deal constitutional settlement was a *fait accompli.*

Judicial vagaries aside, the Commerce Clause fundamentally changed the politics and policy of the minimum wage. The FLSA no longer sought the welfare of women, with its invidious connotations, but the welfare of the economy. The Act applied to 'Labor', to employees within interstate commerce, to every state. It banned sex discrimination and, to meet due process requirements, replaced the equally invidious living wage formula with a flat rate wage set by open debate in Congress. As before, power as well as constitutionalism dictated these details, which suited unions as well as courts. Sheer power dictated the exemption of agriculture, the major employer of African-Americans.

Constitutional language was a more subtle agent of exclusion. Constitutional precepts are usually expressed in skeletal form and interpreted in the courts with narrow legal logic. The structure of the labour market operates by a different logic in which gender and race correlate with occupation. In law, commerce between the states meant just that, transporting or dealing in materials and goods across state lines. The ostensibly neutral FLSA therefore actually benefited workers in the great interstate heavy industries and in transport. These workers were white men. Women, disproportionately in service, retail and clerical jobs, continued to rely on the few gendered state laws to regulate their 'intra-state' employment. Women employed in homes missed out on both, not least because of the colloquial labelling of domestic work as 'service' or 'help'.

The first response of minimum wagers to the inequality wrought by legal language was lawyerly. Case by case they took the definitions to court, bringing groups like cleaners in factories or so called self employed subcontracting home workers under the FLSA by this means. It took the widening reach of the civil rights movement in the 1960s to complete this glacial process. Rights politics touched and changed the minimum wage campaign at its end, as African-American farm workers, the multiracial, unskilled, often female work force in hospitals and schools, the National Committee on Household Employment, found their voice. Displacing back room legal leadership, they took claims for equity to Congress for 'what she or he, like every other American worker deserves'. When Congress put on record in 1974 that 'domestics and the equipment they use in their work are in interstate commerce', the process of definition and inclusion was complete (Hart, 1994, pp.171–2). The individual bearer of equal rights replaced the mother, the employee, the functional citizen of earlier years.

Rights, constitutions, and normal politics

Constitutional politics were inescapable in the United States where all public policy was constructed under constitutional guidelines. In the long run and by comparison with Britain, constitutional imperatives contributed inclusiveness and openness to minimum wage policy. It was not possible, as happened in Britain in 1909, to disregard years of investigation and have a government department run up a new version in ten days, delegating all manner of procedural detail. It was not possible to evade the question of how a wage would be determined and delegate that too to boards in which business could gain the upper hand in private sessions. It was not possible to pass legislation without taking a position at least on direct discrimination. The logic of the universalism of constitutional promises required the constant justification of differentiation and exclusion and created an expansionist momentum, absent in the fluctuations of British coverage. The constitutional text provided a counter claim to powerful interests in the political system, to the indifference of political parties and to legislative decisions which the British sweated worker had to accept. Constitutional authority gave standing and legitimacy to the claims of women in the early phase, workers in the middle years and to excluded citizens in the endgame. Yet the constraints of constitutionalism meant that the development of an adequate policy spread over more than 60 years of frustration and disappointment, creating its own inequalities, in the meantime leaving many sweated workers 'absolutely starved'.

At first glance, Britain did well by comparison, on the dimensions Ackerman (1991, pp.252–4) identifies in his brief comparative discussion. Responsibility and decisiveness were manifest in the direct, speedy and final decision made by Parliament. Transparency was absent as key decisions were stitched up in back rooms and parliamentary deals. But this conclusion holds better for a moment of decision, such as the finalising of the Trade Boards Act of 1909, than for a process of development and implementation over the years. Responsibility was hived off to boards in a massive act of delegation. Accountability to a government department and ultimately to Parliament was attenuated and obscure. Decisiveness was indicted by the campaign's own parliamentary spokesman as allowing ill thought measures to close the debate. The gender-neutral wording, of low paid workers, satisfied accurate socialist claims that sweated labour comprised a class, not a sex. But almost the first trade designated was chain-making, on gendered grounds. Industrial and union power controlled the scope of the legislation and the value of the wage over the years and did not ensure that the neediest necessarily received the benefits. Later, the Thatcher government could end coverage for young people on pragmatic grounds, while the Reagan administration retreated before cries of age discrimination. Only in 1993, facing abolition, did the British find a constitutional strategy and use European treaty obligations to claim that abolition discriminated. In a reprise of the American experience, European workplace rights attack one form of discrimination, by sex, but not another, by race; necessitate expert representation; but nonetheless give access and a claim where political channels have failed. And they change the terms of the debate from the pragmatism of the moment to a systematic justification, from need to right, and from poverty to equity (Hart, 1996).

My evidence has been of the political dynamics of a particular constitution in a particular nation. One more item for the agenda is the extent to which the experience of one polity is transferable. The recent European claim made in Britain is only suggestive of the complexity of the answer. But one clear difference is that American reformers lived in a constitutional culture, shaped by a particular national and historical experience. Further research may determine where this constitutional culture lies on a spectrum from the exceptional to the universal, but a certain fact of this case study is that thinking and strategising in constitutional terms was second nature to American minimum wagers and not just to the politicians and lawyers among them. A future for rights and for constitutional politics in Britain involves learning and change in the polity as well as the better trodden academic fields of discussion of entrenchment in British law or borrowings from the American experience. The constitutional swings and roundabouts in America changed the law but also changed the mobilisation of minimum wagers. Each era had its own leadership, its distinctive coalitions, and its own language. Particularly after the 1920s, the campaign was often remote and obsessed with technicalities which were neither readily comprehensible nor inspiring. The accessibility and self-affirming qualities of rights enhanced democratic politics by comparison with all the constitutional claims which preceded it. This may be a transferable lesson; it is certainly a warning that constitutional politics are as likely to be technocratic as democratic. More likely so where no constitutional culture instructs citizens that they have rights.

The evidence of minimum wage policy history blurs the line drawn between constitutional and normal politics by Bruce Ackerman. This account suggests that the constitutional settlement is continuously contested from all sides and by more than professionals. The minimum wage campaign in the United States was not a movement of the kind Ackerman envisages, engaging in episodic constitutional politics at transformative moments. It was a coalition of individuals and organisations active in 'normal' politics – lawyers, politicians, bureaucrats, interest groups like unions and public advocacy groups like the National Consumers' League – and women excluded from much 'normal' political activity by law. In so far as this was interest group politics, the interest was not blindly pursued until it ran up against the constraint of a Court responsible for maintaining the terms of the Constitution. Minimum wagers knew their Constitution and construed their interest and pursued their goal within their understanding of the public purpose legitimated in its higher law. When they challenged the Supreme Court, and legislatures too, as misinterpreting the higher law and departing from their democratic responsibility to implement the purposes contained in the Constitution, their collectivity appears in Ackerman's terms to have become a movement for constitutional change.

Here, as with the rights debate, reconciliation comes from the collapsing of dichotomies and the abandonment of the association of constitutional politics only with occasional transformative eruptions. Not a few of the building blocks of the New Deal transformation had been deliberately laid by minimum wagers over a 30 year period and that transformation itself was a landmark in, but not a closure of their debate over constitutional interpretation and the public purpose. The process engaged in by public and private citizens, institutional players and especially the courts has been dialectical, not episodic. Its momentum has ensured that no appearance of closure has ever been final. The costs and benefits may be arguable, and variable over time. The normality of constitutional politics as an opportunity within normal politics in the United States seems certain.

I ended my book with the thought that constitutionalism might bring nothing more to British social policy than mixed blessings, lesser evils and modest changes, but that E.P. Thompson's important claim that 'the rule of law itself, the imposing of effective inhibitions upon power and the defence of the citizens from power's all-intrusive claims' is an unqualified good, sets the ambiguous record of constitutional politics in a positive light (Hart, 1994, p.182). On reflection, Thompson's passive defended citizens are not what the theory of constitutions as heuristics or the story of the minimum wage campaign are really about. Taken together, they are an effort to spell out a theory and practice of active agency in which constitutions and rights may be flawed instruments to be handled with care, but are instruments and opportunities nonetheless.

References

Ackerman, B. (1991), *We the People: Foundations*, Belknap Press of Harvard University Press: Cambridge, Mass.

Beer, S.H. (1993), 'Reform of the British Constitution: An American View', *Political Quarterly*, Vol. 64, pp.198–209.

Bryce, J. (1888), *The American Commonwealth*, Macmillan: London.

Cortner, R.C. (1968), 'Strategies and Tactics of Litigants in Constitutional Cases', *Journal of Public Law*, Vol. 17, pp.287–307.

Currie, D.P. (1993), 'Written Constitutions and Social Rights,' in Hart, V. and Stimson, S.C. (eds.), *Writing a National Identity: Political, Economic, and Cultural Perspectives on the Written Constitution*, Manchester University Press: Manchester.

Davis, M.F (1993), *Brutal Need: Lawyers and the Welfare Rights Movement, 1960–1973*, Yale University Press: New Haven.

Dicey, A.V. (1905), *Lectures on the Relation between Law and Public Opinion in England during the Nineteenth Century*, Macmillan: London.

Garrow, D.J. (1994), *Liberty and Sexuality: The Right to Privacy and the Making of Roe v. Wade*, Macmillan: New York.

Gilligan, C. (1982), *In a Different Voice: Psychological Theory and Women's Development*, Harvard University Press: Cambridge, Mass.

Glendon, M.A. (1991), *Rights Talk: The Impoverishment of Political Discourse*, Free Press: New York.

Graham, H.D. (1990), *The Civil Rights Era: Origins and Development of National Policy*, Oxford University Press: New York.

Hamilton, A, Madison, J. and Jay, J. (1961), *The Federalist*, first published 1787, Dent: London.

Hart, V. (1992), 'Feminism and Bureaucracy: The Minimum Wage Experiment in the District of Columbia' *Journal of American Studies*, Vol. 26, pp. 1–22.

Hart, V. (1994), *Bound by Our Constitution: Women, Workers, and the Minimum Wage*, Princeton University Press: Princeton.

Hart, V. (1996), 'Redesigning the Polity: Women, Workers, and European Constitutional Politics' in Galligan, B. and Russell, P.H. (eds.), *Redesigning the State*, Federation Press: Annandale, NSW.

Kingdom, E. (1991), *What's Wrong with Rights? Problems for Feminist Politics of Law*, University of Edinburgh Press: Edinburgh.

Klare, K. E. (1977–78), 'Judicial Deradicalization of the Wagner Act', *Minnesota Law Review*, Vol. 62, pp.265–339.

Mansbridge, J.J. (1986), *Why We Lost the ERA*, University of Chicago Press: Chicago.

Minow, M. (1990), *Making All the Difference: Inclusion, Exclusion and American Law*, Cornell University Press: Ithaca.

Rosenberg, G.N. (1991), *The Hollow Hope: Can Courts Bring About Social Change?*, University of Chicago Press: Chicago.

Ryan, A. (1991), 'The British, the Americans, and Rights' in Lacey, M.J. and Haakonssen, K. (eds.), *A Culture of Rights: The Bill of Rights in Philosophy, Politics, and Law – 1791 and 1991*, Cambridge University Press: Cambridge.

Scheingold, S.A. (1974), *The Politics of Rights: Lawyers, Public Policy, and Political Change*, Yale University Press: New Haven.

Tushnet, M.V. (1987), *The NAACP's Legal Strategy against Segregated Education, 1925 –1950*, University of North Carolina Press: Chapel Hill.

West, R. (1988), 'Jurisprudence and Gender', *University of Chicago Law Review*, Vol. 55, pp.1–72.

Williams, P.J. (1991), *The Alchemy of Race and Rights*, Harvard University Press: Cambridge, Mass.

5 Judicial review, democracy and the special competency of judges

John Arthur

The United States[1] is famous for its practice of judicial review, in which judges are empowered to enforce constitutional limits on legislative power. But why, it is often asked, should today's popularly-elected officials be bound by a 200-year-old document, interpreted by unelected judges? Having a constitution, even a written one, is one thing; but it's quite another to give judges the power to interpret it. Why not let the people's representatives decide which laws are consistent with the Constitution and then if the electorate disagrees with their interpretation that opinion can be expressed at the next election? Surely that would be a far more democratic and therefore sounder basis on which to proceed. Or so, at any rate, it is often said.

That familiar line of thought poses an important challenge to the practice of judicial review – a challenge that I propose to take up in stages. First, I shall provide a few brief historical comments on the origins of the practice of judicial review in the United States. Next, I shall consider the claim that judicial review is undemocratic, first by asking what, exactly, is meant by the claim. How, I shall ask, ought we to understand the meaning of 'democratic' in this context? That will lead, in turn, to further reflections on some of the ways that judicial review may be said to be anti-democratic and, finally, to a discussion of the special competence of judges to serve as final arbiters over the Constitution's meaning.

Background

Neither the Bill of Rights nor judicial review was explicitly included in the original US Constitution. Many states, fearful of the power of the new national government and the possibility that it might infringe on their own sovereignty, decided to press for a series of amendments designed to limit the powers of the newly formed Congress and protect individual rights against the national government. The result was that the first Congress passed and sent to the states for ratification what we now know as the Bill of Rights, which are the first ten amendments to the Constitution.

Nor, second, did the original Constitution explicitly call for judicial review as the mechanism by which to enforce those rights, or to enforce any of the other constitutional limits imposed on both the national and state governments, for that matter. 'Federalist Number 78', written by Alexander Hamilton (1787) to urge the adoption of the Constitution, is widely regarded as the canonical account of the role of the judiciary and the meaning of its powers under Article III of the Constitution. 'The interpretation of laws,' Hamilton (1787, p.467) wrote, 'is the proper and peculiar province of the courts. The Constitution is and must be regarded as fundamental law. It therefore belongs to them (judges) to ascertain its meaning.' Hamilton went on to explain the sense in which the Constitution is regarded as fundamental law: 'If there should happen to be any irreconcilable variance between the law and the will of the people, that which has the superior obligation and validity ought, of course, to be preferred to the statute, the intention of the people to the intention of their agents' (Hamilton, 1787, p.467). Hamilton's suggestion is that elected officials are not in fact the holders of sovereign power, but instead are bound by the document enacted by the people as a fundamental charter. In that way, it is the people rather than the elected officials who are sovereign and, further, it is on the people that the explanation and justification of judicial review ultimately depends.

It is far from clear, however, that this suggestion makes sense. In explaining it, we will first consider why people might limit the power of elected lawmakers whom, after all, they chose themselves. While such a practice seems contrary to the values on which democratic government rests, I shall argue that this familiar claim is mistaken and can be seen to be so when we reflect on the nature of those democratic values appealed to by judicial review's critics. First, then, we must ask what, exactly, is involved in the claim that a government 'respects democratic values'?

Democratic values and judicial review

Democratic government is not achieved merely with the introduction of elections: Brezhnev and Stalin were regularly elected by large majorities. What, exactly, kept the old Soviet Union's system from embodying genuine democratic values?

Two points need to be made.[2] First, any genuinely democratic government must be open, in the sense that all those who are entitled to participate are, in fact, allowed to do so. If a government is to embody the ideals inherent in the democratic ideal, neither the vote nor the opportunity to run for office can be arbitrarily and unreasonably denied. Just which people are, in fact, entitled to participate can of course be controversial. In the US we have seen much disagreement about voting age, for example, as well as whether people who neither have children nor own property should be allowed to elect the officials governing school districts, which are financed by property taxes.[3] My point is not that these are simple issues, for plainly they are not; rather it is that inherent in the democratic ideal is the thought that governments must not arbitrarily or unfairly deny members of any group (women and racial minorities come to mind here) the opportunity to participate in the political process, either as candidates or as voters.

The second democratic value, in addition to openness, is fairness: democratic governments must not only allow open participation, but that participation must be on fair terms. By that I mean that political influence and power must be distributed *correctly* among all the participants; giving some people extra votes, for instance, would not be compatible with the democratic value of fairness. As with openness, there is also room to dispute just what fairness requires; not all cases will be as clear as plural voting.[4]

My concern here, however, is not to explore these issues but to point out their constitutional implications. If we assume fairness and openness are (among) the virtues of any democratic system, then the judiciary may be thought to play an important role in promoting democracy. Indeed, not only is judicial review compatible with democracy, but it may in fact be required by it.[5] I will assume that elected officials are sometimes tempted to act in ways that are incompatible with democratic values of openness and fairness since, having won an election, they often hope to stay in office. One of the roadblocks to winning the next election, of course, can be a democratic system's openness and fairness.

Thus, during the 1960s and 1970s, judicial review often served to make the political process both more open and more fair. Openness was encouraged as the Court, relying on the Constitutional guarantee of 'equal protection' of the law for all citizens and its requirement that every state maintain a 'republican form of government', abolished laws imposing literacy requirements on voters[6] and college students,[7] and rejected residency requirements for members of the military who wished to vote.[8] Each of these decisions was opposed by democratically-elected officials, yet each enhanced rather than reduced democratic values.

The Supreme Court also exercised its power of judicial review in order to enhance democratic fairness. One method it used involved re-apportioning districts set up to elect congressional representatives. Population shifts, usually from rural to urban areas, had taken place over the previous years to the point that in Georgia, for example, 50 per cent of the state's population was limited to electing only 10 per cent of its representatives to Congress. Relying on the Constitutional requirement that members of the

US Congress must be chosen 'by the people', the Court overturned such districting schemes, stating that 'one man's vote ... is to be worth as much as another's'.[9] The Court then went on to attack unfair districting patterns at both the state and local government levels. Relying on the equal protections clause, the Court held that it is a violation of the Constitution for a citizen's voting power to be diluted as compared with others. Again, then, we see an unelected judiciary overruling decisions made by elected officials, but doing so in a way that enhances democratic values.

In addition to imposing unequal voting influence, legislators can also undermine democratic fairness by limiting those who would criticise government officials or their actions. Those in power can thus help assure their re-election by preventing opponents from challenging their legislative records, policies and personal suitability for office. Here again, however, the US Supreme Court, under Chief Justice Warren, prevented these legislative abuses of democratic values by seeking to limit government censorship across a wide front. Unless political speech is 'directed to producing immanent lawless action and is likely to produce such action,' the Court said, government can not invoke police power against a critic.[10] In another important case, public officials seeking civil damages for libel and slander were required under the First Amendment's free speech and free press provisions to prove not only that what was said was false but also that it was uttered either with knowledge of its falsity or with reckless disregard of whether it was the truth.[11]

So besides equalising voting power, judicial review can also promote democratic fairness by protecting the rights of critics of government to criticise officials and their policies. Far from working against democratic values of openness and fairness, in these circumstances judicial review can, and has, served to enhance them. Other forms of judicial review, however, seem not to be able so easily to be dealt with from the perspective of democratic values, and it is to those cases that I now turn.

Democratic self-incapacitation

The US Constitution includes many provisions that seem to have little to do with either the fairness or openness of democratic government. It imposes limits on elected officials by banning practices such as 'cruel and unusual punishment', for example, as well as by requiring legislators not to deny citizens life, liberty or property without 'due process of law', to allow the 'free exercise of religion' and to prevent 'unreasonable searches and seizures', among many others. The Supreme Court has often made controversial and sometimes deeply unpopular decisions as it interprets provisions such as these. Because these are substantive rights, not ones required by democratic procedures, the Court's enforcement of its own interpretation of them against popularly-elected lawmakers may therefore seem incompatible with democratic values. Thus the earlier question arises once again: why should courts in a country committed to democratic values be allowed to give the final, definitive meaning of the constitutional limitations imposed on government?

One answer, familiar from the earlier comments by Alexander Hamilton, involves what might be termed 'self-incapacitating rules'. What I mean is this. We are all sometimes tempted to do things that we will at a future time regret. Thus, for example, I tend to turn my alarm clock off and go back to sleep. I might therefore put the alarm clock across the room before I go to sleep, knowing that in the morning I shall have to get out of bed in order to turn it off. By making it more difficult to violate the rule I have set for myself to arise early, I seek to avoid what my 'better self' knows would be a mistake; I incapacitate myself.

Such self-incapacitating rules might be thought to make political sense in various ways. Elected officials, under pressure from constituents, sometimes act in haste, without adequate information, or else out of anger and frustration with events; other decisions may reflect prejudice toward religious or racial minorities that, on further reflection, we would know to be wrong. Because of these tendencies, it might make sense for people to seek to provide constitutional guarantees that serve, in effect, to incapacitate themselves (or, in this case, their elected officials.)

Due process guarantees for people accused of crimes fit neatly into this picture, since it is often tempting to respond to temporary increases in crime or to particularly violent acts by passing legislation under strong political pressure and without due consideration of its consequences. Similarly, we might also think that because there is a dangerous tendency for us to ignore the rights and interests of unpopular religious or ethnic minorities, it might also be reasonable to make it more difficult than normal to enact legislation which harms such groups.

The Supreme Court has in fact read the US Constitution to require such 'self-incapacitation'. Basic constitutional doctrine insists that laws disadvantaging minorities or infringing basic rights be subjected to 'strict scrutiny', which means that legislation must be shown to serve an important purpose that cannot reasonably be achieved by any other means. 'Strict scrutiny' fits easily within the model of self-incapacitating rules designed to require that the legislature has given due consideration to the possibility that its actions may be inconsistent with the ideals of equality and individual rights to which the society is committed. In that sense, as Hamilton observed, the Constitution – as representative of the people's will – is superior to the legislature.

Like Ulysses, who ordered himself tied to the mast, judicial review represents an attempt to insure that the political system is constrained from passing laws that express prejudice or violate rights. Viewed that way, the exercise of judicial review in the name of protecting basic rights and resisting legislative prejudice seems less anti-democratic. Though such limits cannot be defended as a means to enhance the democratic procedural values of openness and fairness, they are nonetheless compatible with the settled, deepest commitments of citizens to protect rights and reject prejudice as well as secure democratic fairness and openness.

It may seem on further reflection, however, that this picture is in fact quite confused. It depends on imagining that 'the people' who adopted the Constitution provide sufficient authority for the Supreme Court to uphold the right to get an abortion and to find that school prayer is unconstitutional. The US Supreme Court has taken just these positions in recent years, in each case against the strong opposition of elected officials and large numbers of citizens. Where, then, is the mythical political 'self', independent of the legislature, that made these unpopular self-incapacitating decisions?[12] In fact, of course, citizens are often unaware of the Court's decisions; or, if they are aware of them, they may strongly disagree with the Court's interpretation. It is therefore far from clear how judicial review can be understood in terms of 'self-incapacitating' rules.

Constitutional interpretation and original intent

One familiar defence of the self-incapacitating model shifts the discussion away from the purposes of judicial review to the debate over constitutional interpretation. It is sometimes argued, in the spirit of self-incapacitation, that the only proper method of constitutional interpretation is for judges to set aside their own values and political principles and defer instead to the specific intentions of the document's framers.[13] Following this line, dissenters in *Roe v. Wade* argued that because the original framers did not think abortion rights were protected under the Constitution the case was wrongly decided.[14] Similarly, defenders of original intent point out, the framers had a fairly narrow understanding of the meaning of 'cruel and unusual punishment', believing it compatible with a variety of practices, including executions, and for that reason, they claim, capital punishment is not unconstitutional. By following the intentions of the framers, it is claimed, judges protect the legitimacy of their authority by enforcing only those self-incapacitating rules that 'the people' themselves originally intended. Judges are not free to inject their own understanding of what would have been reasonable self-incapacitating rules for the people in place of the historical framers of the Constitution, any more than the legislature is free to ignore the limits on *it* that are imposed by the Constitution.

There are many problems with original intent, however, including the problem of identifying who the 'framers' actually were and the fact that many of the framers disagreed among themselves about how best to interpret the document.[15] Even setting those problems aside, it is not clear that original intent can undergird the self-incapacitation approach: why should the current generation be bound by the intentions of long-dead framers? *Their* choice of self-incapacitating rules is a dictatorship by framers that seems no more democratic than one by contemporary Supreme Court justices.[16] Given that, however, the anti-democratic nature of judicial review emerges once again. If original intent cannot save the self-incapacitating model, then how can it be defended against the point that the Supreme Court often overturns laws with wide popular support and strong legislative backing?

Recall first that the framers deliberately chose to include in the Constitution broad concepts like 'due process of law', 'cruel and unusual punishment' and 'free exercise of religion' even though they could have chosen not to do so. Why, we need to ask, might they have done that? One answer is suggested by the historical situation of the framers: as Enlightenment figures, we would expect them to believe in the power of reason to reach sound moral and political judgments, if only it can be brought to bear on problems.[17] Given that commitment, it would make sense for the framers to think that, however much they might believe they had the best account of these general concepts, they might nonetheless be mistaken. Instead of tying later generations to their specific understanding, they would have reasoned, it would be much better to leave them free to pursue the ideals of freedom, equality and due process as they see fit, in light of their own experience and understanding. To do otherwise would run the danger of sacrificing moral progress to the limited, historically-situated understanding of the framers, which is incompatible with the ideals of moral progress and faith in the capacity of reason and experience to enlighten moral reflection.

Having said that, however, the notion of the Supreme Court's enforcing self-incapacitating rules seems all the more troublesome. Granted that the Court's actions are often controversial, and contrary to both the original intent of the framing generation as well as to the wishes of the current majority, are we not led back to the thought that judicial review is antithetical to democratic values? In one sense, judicial review and the Bill of Rights *do* constitute a compromise with democratic values. If it is assumed that all decisions should be made by elected officials chosen in a free and open political process and unconstrained by anything but the fear of electoral defeat, then the US practice of judicial review should be rejected except insofar as in promotes those or other democratic values. Another possibility relies on the idea that people might reasonably reject this absolutist vision of democratic power. Suppose that, like a person employing self-incapacitating rules, the polity in some sense or at some level in fact *wishes* to compromise democratic values, at least to a degree. This desire might, for example, be based on the feeling that majority rule does not provide adequate protection of individual rights and the hope that by limiting democratic processes the right balance between democracy and other values can be achieved. Why would such an electorate not then simply enact a written Bill of Rights and leave it to elected officials rather than judges to decide how best to interpret it, subject only to defeat at the next election? The answer to that important question depends on whether judges are better situated than elected officials to make such judgments, a subject to which I now turn.

The role of the judiciary and the special competency of judges

Two types of argument are available to defenders of constitutional review by judges.[18] The first is a legal argument, and depends on appreciating the nature of the dispute in question. The legislature, we suppose, has passed a law that it believes is compatible with the limits imposed on it under the Constitution; it is not, in the opinion of the majority of the legislators, incompatible with basic constitutional rights. A citizen, however, disagrees and challenges the legislators on constitutional grounds. Perhaps, to take an actual example, the citizen has burned a flag in an act of political protest and has now been charged with violating a state law criminalising 'flag desecration'.[19] Arguing that the First Amendment protects citizens' right to freedom of speech, the citizen disagrees with the legislature's opinion that the Constitution permits such legislation. But now the question arises which branch of government, the legislative or the judicial, should resolve this dispute. The natural answer, Chief Justice John Marshall argued in Marbury v. Madison,[20] must be the judiciary; for to allow Congress to decide in this situation constitutes a breach of the ideal of the rule of law. Members of the legislature are a party to the dispute; they, like the citizen, occupy one of the two positions that is at issue in the case. To allow either party to decide the case thus seems contrary to basic principles of the rule of law.

Not only are judges better situated *legally* to make the decision, they are also *politically* better suited for it, for two reasons. First, federal judges are given life tenure, which insulates them from electoral politics and the need for reelection.[21] As a result, they are better positioned to decide cases on whatever they take to be the merits, independent of political pressure.[22]

Another important political consideration is of greater philosophical interest, as well as more controversial. Though it is important not to overstate the point, it does seem that there is an important difference in the roles of judges and elected lawmakers, which grows out of their diverging political and institutional responsibilities and different roles in the political system. Judicial interpretation and argument demand consideration of justice and morality in ways that legislative activities do not – or at least not to the same extent. Much of what goes on in the US Congress involves hammering out political compromises between competing interests, while debate among judges on the bench involves different sorts of disputes. Edward H. Levi (1964, p.266) puts the point nicely.

[M]oral judgement is frequently involved in the conclusions reached by the judge. Moreover ... the integrity of the process in which the judge is engaged depends not only on distinctions that he may make reasonably, but also on his own belief in the legitimacy and decisiveness of these distinctions. Thus there is an astonishing combination of compulsions on the Anglo-American judge: the duty of representing many voices, of justifying the new application in terms of a prior rule and the equality of other cases, the assumption that reason is a sufficient and necessary guide, the responsibility of moral judgement, and the importance of sincerity – all these tend to give uniqueness to the institution of judicial reasoning in our system and in our society.

Levi makes two important, related points here. First, he points out, legal analysis and interpretation stress the importance of precedent and therefore of consistency, which in turn reflects the ideal of treating similar cases similarly. Distinctions among citizens that a judge makes must, in his terms, be 'reasonable'. Furthermore, says Levi, judicial decisions and the reasoning on which they are based must reflect the judge's 'moral judgement'. This means, as I understand him, that judges aspire to rule in ways that protect the moral and political 'legitimacy' of government. Levi is therefore suggesting that both of these ideals – first, precedent and consistency (expressed as the requirement of justice that similar cases be treated similarly) and second, substantive moral soundness – are central to legal interpretation.[22]

Legislators, of course, should not completely ignore those ideals, but in a democratic system lawmakers are pulled in another direction as well: they must represent the needs and interests of their constituents. Often, therefore, we would expect legislators to feel a conflict between the needs of those who elected them (in the awareness that other legislators are working to protect *their* constituents) on the one hand, and the need to vote for what they take to be consistent with the national or common good on the other. That dilemma is not a minor feature of governments; rather, it is built into any representative democracy. Elected officials must both represent their constituents *and* serve the greater good. Legislators therefore face a pair of dilemmas. Sometimes they confront the choice between doing what will get them elected and acting in accord with moral principle, but they also must sometimes choose between two principles governing their role: doing what is in their constituents' interests and doing what would serve the greater good.[23]

In the case of judges, however, the situation is different. Here we do not expect, or even tolerate, such compromises in principle. Were a judge to admit to voting in a case not on principle and in accord with what the law requires but instead because it was in the interests of an economic, racial or other 'constituency', we would think the judge did not live up to the expectations of the office.[25] Names for such behaviour, such as 'result oriented' and 'biased', carry a stigma for judges that would not be present when applied to a legislator who succeeds in winning a defence contract for her district or increased farm supports for her constituents.[26]

Conclusion

I have argued in this paper that the familiar charge made against judicial review – that it is incompatible with democratic values – can be answered in a variety of ways. Once we are clear on the nature of democratic values we can see that judicial review can, and often does, promote both the openness and the fairness of democratic processes. I next argued that even in cases where the court is not promoting procedural democratic values, judicial review may nonetheless still be compatible with democratic principles. That is because, in protecting individual rights against majority tyranny, judicial review can reasonably be seen to reflect a deeper, more abstract commitment of the people to incapacitate themselves and their democratic representatives. That does not require judges to enforce the specific meaning the framers attached to the Bill of Rights and other guarantees of the Constitution. Nor should judges decide based on what they believe the majority would themselves understand to be the meaning of Constitutional protections designed to give substance to individual rights. Rather, the idea is that judicial review constitutes a sort of 'second-order' commitment of the people to a system that they hope, over time, will lead to decisions that respect individual rights and minimise the corrosive effects of racial, religious and sexual prejudice. There is no *guarantee*, of course, that judges' particular interpretations of basic constitutional ideals like free speech, free exercise of religion and equal protection of the laws will be correct, or even that they will be better than what the people's representatives would have chosen. I have argued, however, that there are important legal and political reasons for thinking that their judgment should be trusted over that of elected legislators. It is therefore possible that, despite disagreements over particular judicial decisions, reasonable citizens might nonetheless remain committed to judicial review and to protecting individual rights against the wishes of elected officials – and, indeed, even against their own wishes.

Notes

1   In the federal system of government used in the US, parallel issues arise at both the national and state levels. Each state of the US has a state constitution that limits and defines the governmental power of the state. As I discuss here, the federal constitution prohibits the *federal*

government from taking specific actions that violate the rights of citizens or powers of state governments. After the US Civil War, the federal constitution was amended to allow the national government to prevent state governments from violating certain rights of their own citizens – much as citizens of countries in the European Union may now go to the Commission of European Communities to challenge statutes enacted by their own governments as being contrary to rights guaranteed by the Treaty on European Union. This paper considers the federal power of judicial review under the US Constitution only, although substantially similar issues arise when citizens ask state courts to rule whether acts of state legislatures pass muster under state constitutions.

2 For a more extended discussion of these issues, see Arthur (1995, Ch. 2).

3 In *Kramer v. Union Free School District*, 395 US 621 (1969) the US Supreme Court held unconstitutional a New York law requiring voters in school districts either to own property or to have children in school.

4 For instance, as I discuss shortly, the US Supreme Court has ruled that electoral districts must be reapportioned to give each vote equal weight. But what about the US Senate, in which each state, no matter what its population, has two senators?

5 This view, that judicial review can serve to 'perfect' the democratic process, is discussed by Ely (1980).

6 *Lassiter v. Northhampton County Board of Election*, 360 US 621 (1969).

7 *Dunn v. Blumstein*, 405 US 330 (1972).

8 *Carrington v. Rash*, 380 US 89 (1965).

9 *Wesberry v. Sanders*, 376 US 1 (1964) at 17.

10 *Brandenburg v. Ohio*, 395 US 444 (1969).

11 *New York Times v. Sullivan*, 376 US 254 (1964).

12 Martin Hollis stressed this point in the question period following delivery of this paper at the UEA Conference. I am thankful to him for impressing on me the importance of this question .

13 Robert Bork defends this view, as does Chief Justice William Rehnquist. See, for example, Bork (1971) and Rehnquist (1976).

14 *Roe V. Wade*, 410 US 113 (1973).

15 Among the many discussions of the problems with original intent, see Brest (1980), Dworkin (1985, Ch. 2), Bassham (1992) and Arthur (1995, Ch. 2).

16 One possibility, which I have discussed elsewhere, is that the current generation has 'tacitly' consented to the framers' original understanding of the Constitution's self-incapacitating rules. See Arthur (1995, pp.26–32).

17 See in this regard Madison's (1787) famous account of the political theory behind the Constitution, 'Federalist Number 10', in which he

argues that government's most important challenge is to control 'factions', by which he means groups of people committed to using political power contrary to the common good and in violation of individual rights.

18 One further objection to judicial review that I have encountered in Britain, though it is rare in the US, is that judges tend to reflect particular, generally conservative, political views, and for that reason should not be given the power of judicial review. Assuming it is true that judges in the UK are overwhelmingly conservative, then the question is, what follows? Two responses are possible: that judicial review should be rejected, or that judges (and lawyers) should be more broadly representative. I can easily imagine someone's arguing that until judges are drawn more broadly from different political camps, US style judicial review should be rejected. If the facts are as described, that may be the correct reply.

19 In *Texas v. Johnson*, 109 S. Ct. 2533 (1989), the Supreme Court held that burning a US flag is a constitutionally-protected expression of free speech under the First Amendment.

20 *Marbury v. Madison*, 5 US 137 (1803).

21 In contrast, in many states, state judges are popularly elected. Devices are often used to reduce political pressure, for instance term limits may be long. In other states judges are initially appointed and then the question put to the voters is simply whether the particular judge should be returned to office.

22 That is not to say, however, that they are free from other pressures. Federal judges in the US South who enforced desegregation rulings by the Supreme Court came in for heavy social and personal criticism that sometimes included ostracism and threats of violence. That many of them could not have won election as judges, had it been necessary, goes without saying.

23 For an more detailed discussion of the nature of law and legal interpretation that extends these points, see Dworkin (1977 and 1986).

24 I do not mean to suggest that the former, as well as the latter, is not itself sometimes a moral dilemma. An unpopular vote may also be the wrong one in the long run since it can mean that in the future a far less responsible legislator has the seat.

25 That is not to say, of course, that judges will not be affected in their thinking by their experiences as members of a particular class, race, gender, or religious group. Awareness of that is an important part of the argument for having more minorities and women on the bench. But appreciation of the role of perspective and moral outlook in judicial decision-making is not to be confused with the further, mistaken, thought that judges are on the bench to represent the interests of their class, religion, race or gender.

26 Richard Bellamy pointed out, correctly in my view, that judges must also compromise with each other and that much negotiating also takes place within the court. I believe, however, that this type of disagreement over matters of principle is compatible with the view I am defending here.

References

Arthur, John (1995), *Words That Bind: Judicial Review and the Grounds of Modern Constitutional Theory*, Westview Press: Boulder, Colorado.

Bassham, Gregory (1992), *Original Intent and the Constitution: A Philosophical Study*, Rowman and Littlefield: Lanham.

Bork, Robert (1971), 'Neutral Principles and Some First Amendment Problems', *Indiana Law Review*, Vol. 47, No. 1, Fall.

Brest, Paul (1980), 'The Misconceived Quest for Original Intent', *Boston University Law Review*, Vol. 60, No. 234.

Dworkin, Ronald (1977), *Taking Rights Seriously*, Harvard University Press: Cambridge, Mass.

Dworkin, Ronald (1985), *A Matter of Principle*, Harvard University Press: Cambridge, Mass.

Dworkin, Ronald (1986), *Law's Empire*, Harvard University Press: Cambridge, Mass.

Ely, John Hart (1980), *Democracy and Distrust*, Harvard University Press: Cambridge.

Hamilton, Alexander (1787), 'Federalist Number 78' in Rossiter, Clinton (ed.) (1961), *The Federalist Papers*, New American Library: New York.

Levi, Edward H. (1964), 'The Nature of Judicial Reasoning' in Hook, Sidney (ed.), *Law and Philosophy*, New York University Press: New York.

Madison, James (1787), 'Federalist Number 10' in Rossiter (ed.), op. cit.

Rehnquist, William (1976), 'The Notion of a Living Constitution', *Texas Law Review*, Vol. 54, No. 692.

Acknowledgement

I wish to thank Amy Shapiro for many valuable discussions, her helpful comments and her unfailing encouragement.

Section Three
DEMOCRACY AND THE
CONSTITUTION OF EUROPE

6   The European Union?

Zenon Bankowski and Andrew Scott

The problem

What do we see when we look at the European Union? We see a developing structure of governance. In this context a variety of different legal, social and political traditions are brought together with the creation of a durable structure for a trans-national free market as its initial aim. This would be a market existing outwith the structure of the sovereign (nation) state. The central point we want to address in this paper is: what questions does this process of integration raise for legal and political theory? How might it transform our way of thinking about law and community?

We observe changes in the process of European integration and these changes present challenges to orthodox notions of legitimacy and law. Law derives legitimacy from the state, and the state derives its authority and validation from the people – the sovereignty of the state is the sovereignty of the citizens of the state and to hold this inviolate is for some an article of democratic faith. The rule of law maintains the existence of the state. At the same time, the existence of the democratic state legitimises the rule of law. Law is always enforced, sometimes by coercion, but more often through acquiescence – by consensus, as in the 'society of law'. In modern states, consensus that the law is morally just underpins societal respect for the law and, by extension, underpins the integrity of the state and the social order itself. When laws do not command consensus – when they are regarded as unjust – the people may not acquiesce and there are problems. The brief (1988–92) poll tax experiment in Britain was a good example.

What we have, therefore, when we conceptualise the moral – indeed, practical – basis on which the rule of law rests is a self-reinforcing, symbiotic relationship between the state and law. Within this relationship it is the democratic process that plays the role of intermediary, mediating between ideological disputes in the political arena and tempering the legislative excesses to which a government might otherwise fall victim. The democratic process ensures that the legislators conform to 'just' and 'fair' procedures as they decree what the law will be. Moreover, the democratic process ensures that a government that enacts laws which are considered to be substantially 'unjust' or 'unfair' will be rejected. Thus, in the modern nation state, the role of the citizen assumes a pivotal position in the legitimation and validation both of the state itself and of the laws enacted therein.

In this essay, our focus will be on the development of European Community (EC) law. In particular, we shall address the theoretical problems raised by the creation and development of a system of law with, seemingly, no grounding in the societies over which it exercises control comparable to the institutional (in the very broadest sense) foundations that together buttress law and society in the modern nation state. At one level the problem is straightforward: unlike law within the modern nation state, the development of European Community law lacks a basis in the concept of a European state that rests securely upon the foundations of a European citizenry. Consequently, there would appear to be no obvious basis for acceptance by the citizenry over whom the law applies, far less their acquiescence. How then is this problem to be overcome? Among a number of proposals advanced to address this problem, we shall consider three. In each case, however, we find these proposals lacking.

The first requires that we acknowledge that, in practice, the legitimation of domestic law is inextricably linked to the process of democratic government – or at least those arrangements that the citizenry of the nation state accepts as constituting democratic government. Consequently, our attention might turn to the arrangements of governance at the European Union level and propose that these too should correspond to the standard tenets of democratic government. To this end one would stress such principles as transparency and accountability in the governance structure, and a legislative process that conforms to standard practices in democratic nation states. Inevitably this would direct us to matters pertaining to the widely acclaimed 'demo-cratic deficit' within the EU, and the proposal of specific reforms to the institutional structure of the European Union that address this deficit. The inadequacy of this approach is implicit in the distinction that Joseph Weiler (1993) draws between 'formal' and 'social' legitimacy. It is a well rehearsed argument that the former might be best enhanced by reconfiguring the institutional arrangements of the EU such that, for example, the European Parliament (EP) acquires greater powers. However, such institution building along conventional federalist lines – or other institutional reforms – would in no sense guarantee that 'social' legitimacy will be enhanced.

Second, we might propose that the legitimacy problem reflects the absence of an explicit Constitutional statement that sets out the aims, and delimits the powers, of that Union – particularly with regard to matters such as 'citizenship'. The suggestion here is that while the Maastricht Treaty introduced the concept of Union citizenship, it said little on what this meant, how it was to be conceived or how it might be operationalised. Some commentators argue that this points to the need for a Constitution with which the citizens of the Union can identify. Once again this appeal to formal Constitution building can be refuted as a remedy because it confuses formal and social legitimacy. Moreover, the Constitutional approach is further flawed by the difficulties associated with the devising of a prior set of socially legitimised rules for entrenching or reforming that Constitution. Beyond this, it is unclear that substituting a legal framework based on formal Treaties by one that is based on a Constitution of citizens' rights would serve to legitimise a process in which such rights might not, in fact, be an issue. Rather, the issue may revolve directly around the policy – or political – process which derives from the Treaties and which would not necessarily be altered by the Union's adoption of a Constitutional base.

A third resolution of the legitimacy problem would be the emergence of a collective EU 'identity' which bore all the characteristics and symbolism associated with European nation 'statism'. This would involve the withering away of national affinities, loyalties and institutions and the emergence, *a fortiori*, of a European 'nationalism' in which formal and social legitimacy were implicit by virtue of the existence of that state. Setting aside the many problems and risks that one might associate with the emergence of a 'nationalist' European state, it is worth noting that there is at least one avenue along which this could develop; through the emergence of a European political culture that reflected the institutionalisation of something akin to European 'party politics' (see Shackleton, 1994). Were this to evolve concurrently with the acquisition of real legislative powers on the part of the EP, then this would represent a credible mechanism for the emergence of a European polity and, consequently, the resolution of the legitimacy problem. For this to be offered as an option, however, a mechanism that facilitates a transfer of ideological debate and activism away from the domestic and towards the pan-European political arena must first be established. For this to occur, a European approach would need to be shown to be superior to an approach from within the domestic political arena – perhaps in the form of a unifying threat or opportunity.

It is clear that, in part at least, the 'legitimacy' problem as outlined above derives from a conventional framework which conceptualises law, governance and policy as coexistent within a single entity in the form of the nation state. This entity is essentially closed – it is sovereign – and one that has few, and manageable, internal contradictions. The stability of the state requires that the architecture of its governance is accepted, and that the rules for modifying that architecture are accepted. Moreover, the state is an exclusive entity. In classical analyses of the nation state, membership of one such order – one state, one legal system, one polity – necessarily excludes the possibility of membership of any other order or state.

An essay that examines questions of legitimacy inevitably tends towards a discussion of sovereignty. When viewed in that light, and assuming that it is not realistic to expect the emergence of a 'new' state on a pan-European basis, the challenge which European integration confronts (as do other instances of international integration) is to overcome the limits implicit in adherence to the notion of the 'sovereign state'. As MacCormick (1995) reminds us, the emergence of the EC as a legal system (a law making system with an 'independent' executive, legislature, and judiciary) has undermined the sovereignty of member states; it is a system of law that can – in those areas in which EC law is competent to act – always trump the national system of law. The conflict of sovereignty arises because of ever more regular collisions between the EC 'legal system' and the prevailing legal order in member states. In examining European integration in general, and EC law in particular, from the perspective of the impact on state sovereignty, it is worth stressing what distinguishes this arrangement from orthodox international agreements which, ostensibly, also compromise the sovereignty of the state. In the latter case, as realist theories of international relations stress, these agreements can, instead, usually be interpreted as responses to emerging (global) challenges to state sovereignty; developments which – if not countered by international cooperation – would effectively weaken the nation state.

With the enlargement (widening) of the EU to embrace the fledgling democracies and infant economies of Central and later Eastern Europe, and with the deepening of EU competencies to include an ever greater number of economic and social policies, the force of the collision between the legitimacy and substantive claims of state law and (versus) EC law is likely to become ever more pronounced. By serving to increase further the extent of economic and social diversity – and divergence – within the EU, widening and deepening can both be expected inevitably to exacerbate the legitimacy problem. The idea of a 'contested Community' in which the judicial arrangements at the Union level become increasingly controversial is, therefore, one that might well describe the future governance of European integration. Even in those instances where EC law presently encounters few legitimacy problems, such as in the law required to sustain the liberal internal economic order which is at the heart of the economic Union, one can expect enlargement to challenge – if not dislocate – the prevailing equilibrium.

The challenge for the EU – if the EU cannot hope to work as a state (which self-evidently it cannot) – is to design an architecture which is fluid enough not to breach the fundamental pillars of the prevailing nation state order, or the principles that underpin these orders, but which is, at the same time, firm enough to bind together different and perhaps divergent nation states to ensure that this new system of law is accepted and acceptable; legitimised and validated. The new arrangement must also be sufficiently robust to withstand externally created shocks and develop coherent policies capable of commanding a broad consensus across the populations of the member states.

The suggestion offered in this paper is that as integration proceeds, increasingly law will need to be considered in a polycentric way and this will involve a consideration of the way different systems interact and interlock and of the relations between normative and territorial space. The question posed concerns the implications for fostering identities that are not based on the nation state but which are probably necessary, as implied above, if the construction of Europe is to be based on a coherent design. Can we construct a European identity and, if so, how might this be done? The challenge for legal theory is to understand an order where the sovereign state no longer has such sway; where group identity counts; where there are many normative systems intersecting with no one system being especially privileged. How is this to be achieved without, to take an extreme example, collapsing into the bureaucratic administrative systems of the old Eastern Europe or the soullessness of fully fledged market capitalism? The task of this chapter is to begin to look for what might become elements of what we might call a new constitutional architecture.

Sovereignty and the process of integration

The change of names can be revealing. We started with a European Economic Community: but recently the word 'Economic' has been dropped and words like 'Community' and 'Union' predominate. We might say that the processes driving European integration have been, over the past three decades, mainly economic but that the impact of the unfolding (economic) order extends beyond the strictly economic arena. Joseph Weiler has documented the process whereby the European Court of Justice has started creating what is effectively a constitutional structure for the European Union. This process has, certainly, been affected by the need to establish economic foundations for the market. This has had implications for the way that fundamental normative questions are addressed by the Court, and thus also for the notions it has deployed of community and unity. Through a radical reinterpretation of the Treaty, the Court has been able to derogate from and bypass the sovereignty of the nation states that composed it. The story of its doing so leads us to question traditional notions of law as essentially state based. Legal theory is thus forced to reconsider its traditional assumptions. What is happening to the sovereign state and municipal law here? A theory that only sees law as state law linked in a system to the sovereign state would have a problem here. It would be ambivalent as to how to describe the system.

For the UK, the *Factortame* case illustrates the problem pointedly.[1] The European Court of Justice (ECJ) ruled that provisions of the Merchant Shipping Act and regulations made by the UK government under it were incompatible with basic principles of EC law. They restricted fishing against EC fishing quotas in British waters to boats substantially British owned. This was found incompatible with freedom of establishment and the free movement of capital. Hence the Act had to be, as it was delicately put, 'disapplied'. The decision seems *prima facie* incompatible with the sovereignty of the UK Parliament, and thus the sovereignty of the British state, as these have been traditionally understood. If EC law overrides Acts passed after due consideration by the national parliament, how can that body or the nation it represents still be sovereign?

One possible answer would be by a combination of self-imposed restriction with delegation. The self-imposed restriction was undertaken through enactment of the European Communities Act in 1972, Parliament thereby restricting itself from future legislation incompatible with EC law except until such time as any Parliament might expressly repeal the whole of the 1972 Act and thereby revoke British membership of the EC. The element of delegation was then one whereby the UK Parliament delegated power to legislate to the EC organs, with valid effect for the United Kingdom during the period of validity of the European Communities Act. On this view, the case does not mark a loss of sovereignty, but simply a delegation of power by a still-sovereign entity. Thus the rules are binding by simple virtue of the fact that the UK Parliament has assented to this delegation. There is still really a single state legal system and all law, even Community law, fits into that system. (The same, presumably, holds good for every other single member state, all of them having chosen a common point for delegation of power.)

But there is a second possible view. It can be viewed from the other side, as it were. The fact that Parliament's legislation can be in effect invalidated implies, surely, a change of sovereignty. On this view we have a situation where the sovereign is a compound of the Community organs in Brussels, Luxembourg and Strasbourg. If this is the case the UK has no longer a sovereign Parliament and is no longer a sovereign state. Sovereignty has passed to the Community. The same is then true of all the member states, and it must follow that the EU is becoming, or has become, a sovereign federal entity.

What is the truth of the matter? From the standpoint of a theory that bases law on some assumption of sovereignty, either answer is theoretically acceptable. For whatever way we look at it, we have a sovereign entity which is the source of the law and defines the system. This has always been the problem with looking at the law from a single system point of view, since a system always seems to presuppose that there will be axioms which will be the start of the system. In law these become translated as the starting points of law – its sovereignty. So one system always seems to crowd out the other – there can only be one system at a time. Therefore we can say either the EU is a sovereign state or the member countries are sovereign. They cannot both be sovereign at the same time. But in this light, what is not problematic theoretically is acutely problematic politically. Sovereignty is a zero sum game, and the great political issue is: who has it? Might it, however, be possible to defuse this political dispute by challenging its theoretical premise? MacCormick (1993) has, in effect, suggested this in challenging the 'monocular' 'self system' view. He suggests abandoning the single system approach. If there were a third viewpoint that can allow for a plurality of systems, each with its own criteria of validity, a pluralistic picture would emerge, in which there would be neither room nor necessity to ascribe sovereignty to a single system or its organs.

The process of constitutionalisation

Is such a pluralistic picture credible? An examination of the process of legal integration in the Community provides an example of the different tendencies at work, from which we can try to answer our original questions.

There does seem to be a unifying legal imperative at work. Weiler (1991) identifies three phases. First, there was, in the foundation period of the Community, a 'constitutionalisation' of the Community legal structure. Four doctrines were important here.

i   The doctrine of direct effect says that Community norms that are clear, precise and self sufficient must be regarded as the law in the countries in which they are being applied. This applies to all actions producing legal effects in the Community. This doctrine is important also because it creates rights not only between member states and the Community but also rights of individuals against state and community and *inter se*.

ii The doctrine of supremacy means that Community norms are superior to municipal norms. But this is not the same as saying, in international law terms, that treaties are self executing, for here the Community norm does not enter the municipal order with an equal normative status; rather, it has superior status. Thus 'lex posterior derogat lex priori' does not apply as between a later national Act and an earlier Community norm. An earlier Community norm will always be superior.

iii The doctrine of implied powers said that where the Community needed powers to further the legitimate ends of the Community, they would be implied.

iv The Court said that it would review Community measures in respect of the violation of human rights.

None of these four doctrines was contained explicitly in the Treaty itself. These doctrines have been elaborated by the Court in a series of decisions which, for Weiler, can only be understood in terms of a federal state.

For our purposes, another important aspect was contained in the Treaty; that is judicial review. The Commission and any member state may, under Articles 169–172, bring an action against another state for failing to fulfil its obligations under the Treaty. More important is the procedure under Article 177 which provides a special procedure for raising judicial review at member state level. When questions concerning the implementation of the Treaty are raised in a municipal court, that court may request a preliminary opinion from the ECJ. This Court looks at it, remits its opinion to the local court, which then gives a decision based upon this. In these cases, it is often an individual litigant who pleads that something should not be applied because it violates Community obligations. Attempts by member states to escape Community obligations therefore, regularly come up before their local courts.

The second phase comes through the transformation of the competencies of the Community. The principle of enumerated powers as a constraint on the Community's material jurisdiction all but disappeared. No core of sovereign power was left beyond the reach of the Community. The important factor here was Article 235:

> if action by the Community should prove necessary to attain, in the course of the operation of the common market, one of the objectives of the Community and this Treaty has not provided the necessary powers, the Council shall, acting unanimously on a proposal from the Commission and after consulting the European Parliament, take the appropriate measure.

This Article was at first interpreted strictly as a codified version of the implied powers doctrine, to compensate for lack of powers within an area explicitly granted by the Community. It later came to be used to produce new powers and new objectives.

The first stage of this constitutionalising process occurred, says Weiler, while political integration was regressing. But it was exactly this regression that allowed the states to accept the harder constitutional discipline. With the legal avenues being blocked, they developed their political control. The politico–legal equilibrium suited the states. For the interplay between the legal and the political regimes gave states positions of power that they could not attain in more traditional international legal orders. The constitutional structure bound the states communally by a strong legal chain. At the same time the power to veto decisions in the Council of Ministers gave each member state a strong say in the process, while the veto power weakened the political system of integration that was intended to propel EC member states towards the 'ever closer union'. It was left to the European Court of Justice to establish a basis from which, later, it would be in a strong position to shape both the speed and the direction of European integration.

In the second phase, when the power of the legal structure was consolidated, the political process also moved in the direction of greater – or deeper – integration. First, there was a revival and something of a 'relaunch' of the Community. We were at the end of the de Gaulle era and Ireland, the UK and Denmark had joined. But most important was that, given the decline in the supranational decision-making power of the Community in the first period, the states had the confidence to go ahead with the massive jurisdictional change. It is important to note here that accepting this was not, as in a federal system, the loss of power to the centre, for the member states had control over the Community decision-making process. They thus had little to fear.

In the final period, with the passing of the single European Act, things again changed. Here we see political power gravitating ever faster to, and in the process transforming the nature of, the European Community. The proximate cause explaining the decision to resurrect decision-making within the Council of Ministers by qualified majority voting (QMV) was, of course, the creation of the single European market. Beyond this, however, it had become clear that, with a Community of 12 member states, the unanimity rule in the Council of Ministers was severely impairing the entire integration process. The subtlety of the White Paper was in the fact that this move was presented as an entirely technical device; showing the uncontroversial ways necessary to arrive at a single market. And there was a further subtlety involved; the willingness on the part of member states to accept QMV was directly related to the Court of Justice ruling in the Cassis de Dijon case which ushered in the 'new approach' to securing the free movement of goods and services. Without the Cassis judgment it is uncertain whether this crucial decision to reintroduce QMV, even over a limited area of matters (see Article 100a), would have been taken.

Consequently, the step to majority voting was taken not as a dramatic step towards a 'New Europe', but rather as a technical necessity to realise the 'non-controversial' objectives of the White Paper – objectives that both promised that material gain would flow to Community citizens and a reorientation of the ideological direction in which European integration was heading. It was thus able to appeal to all sides; supporters of the 'New Europe' and those who supported the free single market. Even Margaret Thatcher was able to accept it! The irony is that the return to QMV, and all that this subsequently has meant for European integration (including the Treaty on European Union), originated in a judicial ruling that all but removed, once and for all, the remaining vestiges of national sovereignty in the economic arena.

What has been presented, by Weiler and others, is a story of the evolution of the Community through the interactions of a range of different actors in the process. We have the emergence of a bureaucratic style of government propelling the Community to ever higher levels of integration whose power was fashioned, first by the founding Treaties and later in the gradual fusion of that bureaucracy with national administrative systems as the competencies and policy responsibilities at the Community/Union level expanded (*pace* Article 235). We might conjecture that the notion of a policy competence being 'shared' between Community and national levels, rather than 'acquired' by the former, has been a useful device in creating and subsequently reinforcing administrative loyalties between Brussels and national centres of government. This might parallel the story of the 'capture' of domestic judiciaries and legal arrangements by the European Court of Justice and EC law which, as we know, was so instrumental in establishing the supremacy of the latter.

More recently, the evolution of European integration has also been driven by a wide ranging debate about the 'democratic deficit'. Both the SEA and the TEU responded, albeit modestly, to calls for greater powers to be vested in the EP in an attempt to redress the balance between the policy authority enjoyed by the institutions of the EU, and the (comparative absence of) transparency and accountability which informed the policy making activities of these institutions. The irony is that part of the reason that the member states were able to countenance power going to the Community was precisely because they would then be able to escape their democratic accountability and political responsibility at home.

What we see developing, then, is a polity that does not follow the old international models. Though the legal architecture of its development looks like a federal one, there are significant differences. There is no popular institution-building and there is no democratic legitimation process in evidence: it is a largely unseen process. There are clearly different normative systems at work here and there is a lot of interaction between them. But the process is not a zero sum game. The devolution of power to the federal centre does not mean that the local power is thereby diminished. This is shown by the arguments that Weiler made for the member states' acceptance of extensive jurisdictional change, and with it far great powers to the Community. The federal drama was not being played here. The member states were so firmly in charge of the Community's political decision-making power that for them these jurisdictional changes were not important – they still controlled power at the centre. Whatever the motives for the outcome we can see that one power system need not crowd out the other.

The procedure of reference to the ECJ under Article 177 is also extremely important in this context. Here we do not get one normative system claiming superiority over the other and thereby absorbing it into its own system. In seeking the reference, the national court is acknowledging that by virtue of the national legal system's own criteria of validity, it is Community norms that are at issue here. The implications of this are far ranging. It widens the circle of actors taking part in the European project and extends its legitimation (in 'rule of law' terms) further to the national level. And this has even broader implications. It means that we can see EU law not as counter to national law but as part of it. From the point of view of judicial review and remedies, this development is powerful indeed. Weiler sees it as to some extent nationalising Community obligations. States can try in all ways possible to escape international obligations but one of the greatest sins, for the Western democracies at least, is to disobey the edicts of their national courts. Moreover, saying that Community law is nationalised does not mean thereby that the local system is supreme and has absorbed the Community system. The acceptance of Community law can be explained by its being inextricably connected with it. Thus one does not have to see any particular system as being sovereign. One might talk instead, of many systems intermeshing and interconnecting, with no particular system's being privileged. It gets away from the foundationalism of sovereignty.

As MacCormick (1993) says, it is the fallacy of foundationalism to suggest that there must be one foundation which is the base of all law. And this is precisely what the legal theory of sovereignty forces us to do: it forces us to look at normative ordering from one perspective, that of some sovereign entity, and to ignore all other forms of normative ordering that occur in everyday life. To abandon the single system fundamentalist model has important political consequences, moving us away from looking at sovereign states as supreme in their own territory. We can look instead at various interlocking systems over the same territory and perhaps dealing with the same people. This new perspective is important when we come to consider European identity and the relations between the different groups in Europe. For we could also apply this way of looking at it to that question also. Thus we might not think in terms of privileging any particular national identity even that of European.

The growth of the EU helps us in this move away from foundationalism because it so clearly threatens the 'sovereign state' view. We have, however, to have a new way of conceptualising the complex series of relationships involved in the growth and development of the EU. Otherwise we might find that the sovereign entity view is not really threatened. Though we might see the gradual collapse of the sovereignty of the member states, it comes to be replaced by EU sovereignty. One way forward is to acknowledge different perspectives or points of view. The criteria of validity will depend upon the perspective we adopt. Looking at the validity of laws from the perspective of the UK system, we will come to a certain set of conclusions as to the validity of laws, including laws that emanate from EC sources. But it will be somewhat different if we look at it from the EC perspective. There, we do not start from the UK parliament or the practice of the legal officials of the UK, but rather from the Treaty and the ECJ and the practice of EC officials. And there we get a picture of what counts as EC law, including sometimes what comes from the member states. No view is thereby privileged; we can thus locate ourselves in different systems depending upon our point of view. No one system will be superior. What we think of EC law *vis-à-vis* municipal law and *vice versa* will depend upon which system we locate ourselves in – what perspective we take. This is the legal scientist's view. But we can go further than this. We can look at the whole EU and its various systems and try to describe them so as to get a sort of 'view from nowhere' – without looking at it from any one point of view. We can use here the idea of what Boaventura de Sousa Santos describes as 'interlegality'. Santos (1987, pp.293ff) says:

> Legal pluralism is the key concept in a post-modern view of law. Not the legal pluralism of traditional legal anthropology in which the different legal orders are conceived as separate entities coexisting in the same political space, but rather the conception of different legal spaces superposed [sic], interpenetrated and mixed in our minds as much as in our actions, in occasions of qualitative leaps or sweeping crises in our life trajectories as well as in the dull routine of eventless everyday life. We live in a time of porous legality or of legal porosity of multiple networks of legal orders forcing us to constant transitions and trespassings. Our legal life is constituted by an intersection of different legal orders, that is by interlegality. Interlegality is the phenomenological counterpart of legal pluralism and that is why it is the second key concept of a post-modern conception of law. Interlegality is a highly dynamic process because the different legal spaces are non-synchronic and thus result in uneven and unstable mixings of legal codes.

We do not have to go along with 'postmodernism' in the legal world, to realise the usefulness of this concept. For this 'shifting porous world' is precisely the world of the EU and the various actors therein. But there is more to the view from nowhere than that. It is not just a question of describing each system without ascribing superiority, one to the other. In alternatively switching viewpoints from one to the other there would not be a view from nowhere but rather a view from 'no particular where' or from all 'wheres' in turn. We must try to find a way to describe the phenomena embracing them all, not in a series, as it were, but rather as a whole.

The EU and community

We have been looking at some developments in the EU that might move us nearer to the aspiration of community with which it started out. This project might also imply the decline of sovereignty and the idea of law as being coupled exclusively with state sovereignty. Instead, we might have interlocking sectors. But what would the implications of this change be for the law of the EU? What form of law does what we have been talking about imply? Can we discern it within the normative order that we have above seen the Court and other actors to be forming?

On one reading the problem revolves around a straightforward collision between morality and the market. The ECJ and the system of EC law need not be legitimised through a political process if the substance of that law enjoys self-evident justification. That is, if there is a coincidence between what individuals and the constituent societies consider to be morally right and what the law dictates to be correct. It might be argued that, in so far as the role of the ECJ was to uphold the principles and practice of the unfettered operation of market forces, and in so far as the unfettered operation of market forces was universally endorsed, then the legitimacy of European law within that specific orbit was implicit. Providing for any departure from universality in support for the unfettered operation of market forces; providing for any activity on the part of the ECJ that interferes with the free operation of markets; or providing for an extension of the rulings of the ECJ beyond matters pertaining to the operation of markets will each expose the activities of the ECJ to the need to be legitimised. We have reached precisely such a stage.

How then can an organisation which was set up as a common *market*, whatever the reasons for that, express another, more communitarian, view? Can market terms express something that seems to go beyond the market? How can what seem to be substantive rights be produced from the formal rights and duties needed to run the market? Thus the formal rights and competencies that are needed to set up the framework and possibility of the market, clash with the more substantive policy issues that are also used to found rights. This, then, is why, in the reasoning of the ECJ, substantive points tend to be dressed up in formalist terms. This is not hypocrisy. The Court is trying to come to terms with all the views in the multilogue. That is why the clashes will intensify; not because of the formal competencies that are being discussed, but, rather, as an effect of the particular substantive issue. Take the proposed ban on tobacco advertising. Is this really a case of unfair competition and therefore within the competencies of the organs? Or is it a substantive issue of health policy? The Court starts from the original vision of the *market*.

In this context, Coppel and O'Neill (1992) have argued that the ECJ has not taken fundamental human rights seriously. The ECJ, they argue, has employed them instrumentally in order to speed the process of European integration. It has not been interested in them for their own sake. The best way of interpreting this sort of contention is not to ascribe intentionality to the Court *per se*. Rather, we should look at the use a particular sort of institutional vocabulary makes of the terminology of fundamental rights and the effects of that.

Grogan is an important case to consider in this respect.[2] In 1989 SPUC (the Society for the Protection of the Unborn Child) brought a case in the Republic of Ireland against various office bearers of the Student Unions there. It sought an injunction to prevent their distributing information and literature about abortion clinics and the availability of abortion in Britain. The case was referred to the ECJ under Article 177. According to Advocate-General van Gerven,

> [T]wo rules which stem from fundamental rights come into conflict in this case: the freedom of the defendants in the main proceedings to distribute information, which I have accepted as being the corollary of the Community freedom to provide services vested in the actual providers of the services .... and the prohibition to assist pregnant women, by providing information which, according to the Irish Supreme Court, results from the constitutional protection of unborn life.[3]

The Court translated what for the Irish Constitution was a fundamental human right into Community legal terms. There it was seen as a restriction on abortion which was defined as 'a medical activity which is normally provided for remuneration [and] may be carried out as part of a professional activity'. It was thus a 'service' under Article 60 of the Treaty. Article 59 prevents any restriction by member states on the provision to provide services throughout the Community. On the particular facts, however, it was held that the injunction was not in breach of EC law.

There are two considerations for us here. There is the relation between what local communities consider fundamental and what the EU legal system considers so, and there is the relation between fundamental rights in an moral/ethical sense and the rights fundamental to running a market. Phelan (1992), and Coppel and O'Neill (1992), see the Courts as translating fundamental rights into economic rights. Thus the universalism of human rights becomes the contingency of economics. Rights no longer trump, but are contingent on the running of the market. They say that in the end the rights discourse of the ECJ is something that takes as fundamental the economic freedoms that are the pillars of the EC. It is those that trump everything. Thus what local jurisdictions see as fundamental will be trumped by this economic vocabulary. It is in this sense that, for them, the ECJ does not take human rights seriously, for it is promoting the economic freedoms as fundamental. In so doing, when it comes to what it sees as local derogations from these, it will override them.

> [I]t should be borne in mind that the principles of free movement of goods, together with freedom of trade as a fundamental right, are

general principles of Community law of which the Court ensures observance.[4]

In this way the ECJ will promote European Integration and forget about Human Rights.

One way of reading this development is that the dangers of the Eastern European road are being realised. Instrumentalisation of law is arrogating power to the Community – and history repeats itself. But that would be too straightforward a reading. It might be argued that these so called fundamental rights are themselves contingent and substantive. What are called economic rights are in fact related to keeping the market going as an efficient and fair entity, and these can be the only true universal rights. One can see some truth in both of these propositions. Economic rights in the sense of those that are geared to the efficient running of the market might go much further than Phelan might think. It might be argued, for example, that equality is necessary for this sort of efficiency. These rights must be distinguished from rights which are economic in the sense that they stem from a utilitarian or economic analysis of law. On this view, the former have universalising tendencies and the latter, particular and substantive.

Here again we come back to the different visions of the Community. In many ways the frozen vision of the Community that Weiler (1994) says we have is one of a single market. It gives us peace and quiet, prosperity and, as we saw, has a strong universalising tendency. The Court tries to implement this vision in extending this framework. But in so doing it extends its own scope. It cuts a swathe through various particularities, obliterating them in the name of market freedoms. Historically this has been no bad thing. Even now, we may see the *Grogan* case as promoting not merely freedom of trade but the freedom of women. So, putting local constitutions in danger might not necessarily be a bad principle.

But the ECJ is not just managing a system. It is, as Weiler (1991) says, promoting it. It is therefore interventionist in two ways. It is intervening to promote a system and, at the same time, it is running a system whose job it is to produce a trans-national efficient economy. These two functions get mixed up. The way the Single European Act was presented illustrates this point; it was presented as a list of technical adjustments to the running of the single market. Thus it was at the same time interventionist and a strong step in a universalising tendency. There is a certain logic to what is happening here, for the instrumentalisation of law in order to produce a formal rational legal system suited to a free market gives rise to rights that will be couched in these terms. This process has particular universalising tendencies and leads to the sort of Community that Weiler has characterised as idolatry.

Conclusion

In this paper we have attempted to elaborate a number of elements which together amount to rethinking the design of the project of European integration. At the heart of our analysis is the problem of sovereignty and the rule of law. Classical notions of law – law as state law – are increasingly redundant when applied to the EU. On the one hand, EC law lacks the apparatus whereby it can be legitimised. That it is implemented and enforced through national courts is, in our view, inadequate as a modality for legitimation, for it ignores the domestic (Parliamentary and, by convention, democratic) mechanisms whereby national law is made. Moreover, increasingly EC law is encroaching beyond the market. It can no longer therefore, if ever it could, be construed as commanding moral authority. On the other hand, and unlike conventional international law, European law does not restate and reinforce the constitutional sovereignty of the nation state; it effectively weakens that sovereignty – an aspect in which present developments in the EU stand in stark contrast to the early years of the EEC. As Milward (1992) has suggested, one of the main consequences of the development of the EEC during the foundation period in the 1950s was that, in effect, it provided a framework to 'rescue' the (sovereign) European nation state from the calamitous excesses of unbridled nationalism.

However, it is not only the extension of the powers of the ECJ – and the subsequent crisis of legitimacy of the law – that is problematic, although this is an important element. In addition, there are sub-national forces from within the polity of EU member states seeking both identity and political expression. In part this is a consequence of the weakening of the sovereign state as the process of integration proceeds. In part, too, it arises from the success of the EU in creating a whole to which social groups can belong that is essentially different from the sum of its component parts. In this reading, the end of the sovereign nation state is upon us. If this transition continues, how best can it be managed? If there is an identity to be forged that is in part European, in part national and in part local, how can a legal order that respects these different orders and which does not exclude any be managed? A deeper examination of the principle of subsidiarity might throw some light on this question.

It is commonplace in some writings on the issue of European integration to confuse the present problem of EU legitimacy with the conditions and requirements of classical nationalism. That is, to regard the EU as being defective as a state due to the absence of the accepted symbolic dimensions of state power; dimensions which, as Krasner (1984) says, 'sustain the ethical and moral needs of citizens, not just their material ones'. In this quote, as in the works of others writing in this vein, one detects a sense of pessimism for the 'European project' on the basis that ethnic and nationalist differences between the peoples of Europe militate against the emergence of a European nation state – that arrangement regarded as necessary in terms of stability. But is the rise of a European nation state necessary for the community of Europe to function effectively as a larger political entity? Some think so. For instance, Laffan (1995):

> nationalism's symbiotic relationship with state power endows it with a central role in legitimising political power within state boundaries which in turn makes the legitimation of European and internationalised governance structures highly problematic.

and Anthony Smith (1992):

> Here lies the new Europe's true dilemma: a choice between unacceptable historical myths and memories on the one hand, and on the other a patchwork, memoryless scientific 'culture' held together solely by the political will and economic interest that are so often subject to change. In between, there lies the hope of discovering that 'family of cultures' ... through which over several generations some loose, over-arching political identity and community might gradually be forged.

We suggest that such gloomy predictions concerning Europe's future mask are in some sense a misinterpretation of the prevailing dynamics of social change. Common to both is that they tend to underplay the extent to which the classical sovereign state is itself no longer viable – and this regardless of European integration. Moreover, in the above citations the 'state' is assumed: the 'power of the state' is implicit. Certainly devising modalities that accommodate multiple cultural societies other than the exigencies of the 'common market' is the difficulty. But it is not a difficulty that would disappear if only the 'European project' would disappear. The true nature of the problem is not *per se* the legitimation of the European Union, although this is part of it: it is to construct a theoretical framework in which different identities and different legal orders can coexist. We must take up this challenge and begin the debate about a future for Europe. We must rest it on a firm ethical base.

We will conclude with a brief mention of a worrying tendency in present developments which seek to address the crisis of legitimacy: the trend towards proposing a 'Europe' of variable geometry. That is, a system of integration in which the legitimacy problem is managed by the participation of member states in only those aspects of the complete arrangement which they consider acceptable to a domestic constituency. In other words, an arrangement whereby membership of the European Union does not automatically involve membership of all aspects of that Union. This is, of course, a 'Europe' of opt outs.

In practical terms, what we would have is a Union which had a number of discrete, albeit overlapping, legal and policy communities nested within it. For the European Union, the core would involve the central four economic freedoms stipulated in the founding Treaty of Rome – the free movement of goods, services, capital and labour – with any common measures beyond this being optional. The notion of variable geometry is appealing on a political level, at least superficially. It suggests an approach in which sovereignty and legitimacy are divisible – to be given in part, and in part retained. But the risk is that this will institutionalise a divided Community – a contested Community. The institutional unity that has, since the beginning, been at the heart of European integration would be destroyed. With this would go the solidarity and search for cohesion that was foremost in the minds of those who designed the institutional architecture of the European project. If institutional unity is compromised, then so too will be solidarity and cohesion. The danger is that fragmentation would follow and the structure that is the European Union would be progressively dismantled. It is not clear what, if anything, would replace that structure.

Notes

1 *R v Secretary of State for Transport, ex. p. Factortame* [1991] 3 All ER 769 (Case C221/89) CJEC.
2 *Society for the Protection of the Unborn Child Ltd. v. Grogan and Others,* [1991] 3 CMLR 849.
3 Opinion of Advocate-General of 11th June 1991, paragraph 25.
4 Case 240/83, *Procureur de la République v. ADBHU* [1958 ECR 520 521].

References

Coppel, J. and O'Neill, A. (1992), 'The European Court of Justice: Taking Rights Seriously?', *Common Market Law Review,* Vol. 29, pp.669–92.
Krasner, S. (1984), 'Approaches to the State: Alternative Conceptions and Historical Dynamics', *Comparative Politics,* Vol. 16, pp.223–46.
Laffan, B. (1995), 'Identity, Legitimacy and Political Order in Europe', paper presented to conference *The European Union and a Changing European Order,* Loughborough University, March.
MacCormick, N. (1993), 'Beyond the Sovereign State', *Modern Law Review,* Vol. 56, pp.1–19.
MacCormick, N. (1995), 'Sovereignty, Democracy and Subsidiarity' in Bellamy, R., Bufacchi, V. and Castiglione, D. (eds.), *Democracy and Constitutional Culture,* Lothian Foundation Press: London.

Milward, A. (1992), *The European Rescue of the Nation State*, Routledge: London.

Phelan, D.R. (1992), 'The Right to Life of the Unborn v. Promotion of Trade in Services: The European Court of Justice and the Normative Shaping of the European Union', *Modern Law Review*, Vol. 55, pp.670–89.

Santos, Boaventura de Sousa (1987), 'Law: a Map of Misreading', *Journal of Law and Society*, 14, pp.279–99.

Shackleton, M. (1994), 'The Internal Legitimacy Crisis of the European Union', *Europa Institute Occasional Paper*, 1, University of Edinburgh.

Smith, A. (1992), 'National Identity and the Idea of European Unity', *International Affairs*, Vol. 68, pp.55–76.

Weiler, J.H.H. (1991), 'The Transformation of Europe', *Yale Law Journal*, 100, pp.2403–83.

Weiler, J.H.H. (1993), 'Parliamentary Democracy in Europe 1992: Tentative Questions and Answers' in Greenberg, D. et al. (eds.), *Constitutionalism and Democracy: Transitions in the Contemporary World*, Oxford University Press: Oxford.

Weiler, J.H.H. (1994), 'Fin-de-Siècle Europe' in Dehousse, R. (ed.), *Europe After Maastricht: An Ever Closer Union?*, LBE: Munchen.

7 Citizenship in the Constitution of the European Union: rhetoric or reality?

Carole Lyons

Introduction

This paper will explore the nature of European Union citizenship in the context of the constitutionalisation[1] of the EC/EU. The concept was formally introduced by the Treaty on European Union (TEU) and presents many problems in its current state. Under the TEU, citizenship of the EU was granted to all nationals of EU member state countries, introducing changes to the EC Treaty which now contains a revised Article 8 detailing the beneficiaries and rights of citizenship. This is an important symbolic development in the evolving constitution of the Union; a formal recognition of the extra-economic character of the EC/EU. But an examination of its substance reveals EU citizenship to be disappointingly feeble and gives rise to questions concerning its nature and limits. Is it an inalienable right granted to all existing and future member state nationals? Could an EU citizen be deprived of this status by a state's choosing to end its membership of the Union? The relationship between nationality and citizenship is also crucial. As member states have different methods of determining nationality it could mean, for example, that an Irish American may be able to avail herself of EU citizenship but a Turkish national who has lived all her life in Germany may not. Since there are approximately 10–15 million legally settled non-nationals in the EU, the fact that they should be further disenfranchised is of concern. The relationship between citizens' rights and human rights has been of interest since the drafting of constitutions in the late 18th century; it is indicative that this problem also remains unresolved in relation to this new citizenship which emerged from Maastricht.

Citizenship, nationality, and human rights are all crucial to the future development of the Union. They are the weapons in the larger battle which has shaped and will continue to determine the personality of that Union; the division between member state sovereignty and a supranational Union. This paper will locate the issues in this overall context and examine the particular difficulties which they raise.

Citizenship

Citizenship is an instrument of both inclusion and exclusion – it serves to determine those who 'belong' and also acts as a 'powerful instrument of social closure' (Brubaker, 1992, p.23). From the initial development of the concept in the Athenian state the emphasis, or indeed whole purpose, of citizenship was the identification of a specific group of people with superior rights. The concept of *citoyen*, which was perceived as being inclusive during the French revolutionary period was, however, also élitist in conception. In creating the revolutionary *citoyen* its authors also created the foreigner and in addition introduced an inherent discrimination attached to citizenship – the active citizen versus the passive citizen. These distinctions were founded upon class and economic considerations; only the active – i.e. tax paying, property owning (male) – *citoyen* could participate in political life. It is undoubtedly trite to recall the dominating race and gender implications of citizenship but it is interesting to observe the extent to which economic factors infiltrate the notion of citizenship from its early development to the definition of European Union citizenslip. Citizenship, as well as clearly delineating a group of privileged persons entitled to certain rights, generally implied that these privileges were economically predicated – land ownership and/or the ability to make tax contributions were the usual criteria in the modern state (which clearly excluded, for example, women and slaves). The very declaration of citizenship has almost always been defined by its denial to certain people.[2] The relationship between citizenship and the construction of the identity of the modern state is also important; a state is defined, constituted and empowered by its citizens – they belong to and may be controlled by it. The state's legitimacy is derived from its *demos*; in the contract that is citizenship, allegiances are demanded of citizens and limited rights granted in return. Citizenship also serves to legitimate the power and governance of the grantor.

Background to EU citizenship

From these essential attributes[3] it is interesting to observe the nature of European Union citizenship, which was introduced by the Treaty on European Union (TEU) in 1992 ('the Maastricht Treaty'). As will be seen, this new 'citizenship'[4] does conform to certain of the traditional standards, arguably the most negative ones. It is economically dictated; defined so as to exclude; and contains unlisted duties. Indeed, the rights attached to it are so limited that it must be questioned whether its only justification lies in increasing the legitimacy of EU institutions and in acting as a mere sop in the campaign which seeks to construct a loyalty to the EC/EU.

The very foundations of citizenship are based on discrimination, privilege and deliberate exclusion. EU citizenship in this sense is not exceptional. If anything, EU citizenship has highlighted and increased the discrimination already inherent in the most tangible rights attached to citizenship – the 'free movement of persons' provisions of the EC Treaty. As will be seen below, these issues have already been argued before English courts and although an outcome is still awaited, the cases themselves serve not only to expose the extent to which EU citizenship is discriminatory but also show how it might possibly provide the means to remedy these faults.

Citzenship's potential – perhaps unforeseen at the time of the drafting of the TEU – is evidenced by the fact that citizenship rights have so quickly been seized upon by litigants. There is little doubt that Article 8 EC was introduced in a blatant attempt at creating a semblance of democracy in the Union, as if placing a 'people'-flavoured icing onto the Treaty cake would solve the long-running and fundamental problems of EC/EU democratic legitimacy. Not all commentators are sceptical of Article 8 and its effects and it may well prove, with the cooperation of the ECJ, to be a significant element of further European integration. However, any hopes that a loyal *demos* would emerge after November 1993 (after the TEU entered into force) would have been overly optimistic, due to the inadequacy of the rights attached to the new concept. It is now widely accepted that progress in EU integration rests most fundamentally upon increased identification between the people who reside in the Union and the institutions which serve it and a related decrease in the alienation which integration has thus far produced. However, if EU citizenship represents the most serious attempt to achieve these objectives, then the exercise is flawed from the outset.

It may well be that citizenship will serve as an external identifier.[5] It may also salve the conscience of the institutional machine to think that 350 million people now legitimate it. Whether it has had any impact upon the people it was supposed to benefit is doubtful, however.[6] The notion that European integration should be accompanied by a concept of citizenship was not altogether novel at the time of the drafting of the TEU.[7] The term 'Citizens' Europe' had been in circulation on an irregular basis since 1974, and rights conferred mainly under the EEC Treaty (1957), together with related jurisprudence, had created some elements of citizenship (see further Durand, 1979 and Evans, 1984). However, the TEU – ironically because it is arguably the least integrationist of the founding Treaties – provided the opportunity formally to introduce EU citizenship. The initiative was that of the Spanish government delegation and received the support of the European Commission and some member states, although others regarded it as vague or premature (see Closa, 1992, p.1154). However, as Closa (1992, p.1157) indicates, 'citizenship was not a very controversial topic' and one might justifiably imagine that the relatively paltry provisions[8] which were introduced may have been regarded as merely declaratory and as having little substantive significance by most of the member states.[9] Yet it may, if only on a symbolic level, be regarded as a meaningful gesture in the overall context of European integration that the fundamentally economic basis of the Communities has been exceeded and this overtly political aspect included in one of the founding treaties.[10]

The revisions introduced by the TEU resulted in the inclusion of a revised Part Two in the (renamed) EC Treaty, consisting of one Article (Article 8). In addition, there was a reference to citizenship in Article B of the Common provisions of the TEU itself which states that amongst the objectives of the Union shall be '... the protection of the rights and interests of the nationals of its Member States through the introduction of a citizenship of the Union' (Article B TEU). The fact that citizenship is referred to in the two Treaties creates some confusion as to whether its application is to be confined to the sphere of activity of the EC Treaty or extends to the wider Union. Some symbolic relevance might possibly be attached to the location of the citizenship provisions in the Treaty, which suggests that they may be regarded as substantive and not merely declaratory (Closa, 1992, p.1158). The European Commission adds credence to the fundamental character of citizenship and its associated rights by suggesting that '[t]he rights flowing from citizenship of the Union are in effect granted constitutional status by being enshrined in the Treaties themselves'.[11] The notion that Article 8 creates rights which go beyond the mere declaratory has received some endorsement in a judicial context[12] and, as a result of a reference to the ECJ arising from this case, that Court will have an opportunity to consider the nature of EU citizenship.[13]

Definition of EU citizenship

Whatever the declared status of citizenship, it is in examining the contents of Article 8 that more critical questions may be posed which expose the relatively threadbare character of the substance of the rights and the devalued nature of its meaning.

Consider first the definition of EU citizenship; Article 8 (1) reads 'Citizenship of the Union is hereby established. Every person holding the nationality of a Member State shall be a citizen of the Union.' Citizenship was, as it were, granted or bequeathed to the incumbents. It is not apparent whether there is anything facultative about this new citizenship; it is imposed upon nationals of the member states without any indication of a consensus element in this significant development.[14] In this regard EU citizenship begins on a conservative note recalling and reinforcing the notion that citizens are created to define and empower the polity.[15]

A more petty contradiction raised by the definition is whether it is in fact EC/Community citizenship or Union citizenship; it is specifically declared to be 'of the Union' but the rights are seemingly limited to the EC Treaty. This is potentially important in at least two respects: human rights are specifically mentioned not in the EC Treaty but in the TEU (Article F. 2.); and citizens are denied participation in important spheres of activity of the Union (i.e. external affairs under Title V TEU (the '2nd Pillar') and justice and home affairs under Title VI ('3rd Pillar')).

What may also be noticed about this brief definition of citizenship is its awkward acknowledgement of the notion that member state sovereignty is being infringed upon in the concession to the superior position of the member states. Why is the definition of *Union* citizenship to be dependent upon the whims of an individual member state? If a comparison, perhaps more anticipatory than real, is made with federal structures elsewhere, then for the central authority to be deprived of the power to determine who shall constitute the people of the federation as a whole represents a unusual division of competencies. There are historical precedents for this, of course,[16] but not in recent times. This is the kernel of one of the most fundamental issues of European integration; the division of competence between member states and the Community/Union. Nationality and citizenship constitute the very essence of sovereignty and it is not difficult to understand why Article 8 did not provide for EU citizenship to exist without the link with member state nationality. This link was re-enforced by the Declaration on Nationality attached to the TEU.[17] As d'Oliveira (1993, p.628) remarks: '[t]he right to decide who is a "national of a Member State", if won by the EC, may harmonise the concept of "national", but paradoxically, will also be the end of the Member States; their sovereignty and existence are jeopardised'.

Nationality may prove to be a fertile ground for future conflicts and is one way in which member states may exert enormous influence over the future of the Union. As long as member state discretion remains absolute in the area of nationality, they will be able to determine the future inhabitants of the Union.[18] This could be exercised either negatively, by states' having restrictive nationality or naturalisation laws, or more positively; the examples of Macau and Hong Kong respectively serve to demonstrate existing contrasting practices. There even exists the possibility for member states to adopt a wide definition of nationality which might affect economic considerations in the Union – for example the granting of Irish nationality to Irish Americans or Spanish nationality to Latin Americans. However, these possibilities must be seen in the context of the fact that 18 million East Germans entered the Community market following the unification of Germany without objection from other member states. Should a member state choose to 'abuse' its nationality powers, Article 5 EC may possibly be exercised against them.[19] What, however, would be the status of EU citizens whose states (or part of a state – Greenland, for example) opts to leave the

Union? Citizenship rights are lost as a result, which must cast doubts upon their 'fundamental' character.

A definition which leaves the member states as the privileged actors in citizenship rights inherently provides an uncertain future for the beneficiaries of such rights and means that EU citizenship, one of the fundamental pillars of future integration, is subject to member state action. If member state control in this context could be regarded as a method of retaining sovereignty or decreasing the 'democratic deficit' it might be understandable, but this is far from obvious.

However, problems with the very definition of citizenship call into question the motivations underlying the introduction of citizenship provisions into the Treaty; the most likely answer in a generous light is a jumbled combination of a desire to create some allegiance with the Union and to reinforce 'people's' rights. Allegiances or loyalty can hardly be constructed – an elective citizenship (promising a decrease in powerlessness) would have been a more appropriate measure to achieve this end. If there was a genuine desire to create or reinforce rights it seems strange that rights which derive from the Union/Community and its separate legal and economic order are dependent upon and can be terminated by a member state's actions. It has obviously always been the case that individuals derive benefits from and participate in Community existence only via their member states and to the extent that the state desires,[20] and while there is still a prospect of a member state's leaving the Union,[21] however unrealistic this may be in practice, it highlights the precarious nature of individually exercised rights.[22] Underlining this essential element of EC/EU construction is the Article 8 definition – as long as the member states remain in control of the *demos*, the Community/Union will remain secondary and integration a reversible process. There is here a question to be asked concerning fundamental (human) rights, however; if a direct connection is to be made in the future between EU citizenship and human rights, the standing of such rights will be at issue if a member state may deprive one or all of its nationals of same – how fundamental can they be in this case?[23]

Citizenship duties

Citizenship as a political tool has an inherent attraction for conservative forces in any society, given the identification of a people with a polity and the latter's right to demand allegiance or duties because of this citizenship link. In this regard EU citizenship conforms to the traditional notion of the concept, as Article 8 (2) reads 'Citizens of the Union shall ... be subject to the duties imposed [by the Treaty]'. Considering the extent to which nationals of member states were allowed any form of vote on the inclusion of Article 8 in the EC Treaty, this wording must be regarded as a breach of democratic trust at the very least and negates the notion that Article 8 exists to decrease sentiments of powerlessness and exclusion in the EC/EU. What kinds of duties are at issue? They are still to be detailed, but it is indicative that this remains a potentially more expansive aspect of citizenship than the weak rights which are listed. Duties which may be conceived are the duty to pay taxes or the duty to take part in EU defence activities. Both of these possibilities are problematic; people other than EU citizens are required to pay taxes yet are excluded from citizenship-related rights; a duty to fight in an EU army or undertake military service at that level would be objected to not least by the nationals of those militarily neutral member states.

Citizenship rights

When the specific rights attached to Union citizenship are examined, it further emerges as a problematic innovation which will require substantial revision, if it is to be seriously considered as forming one of the foundations of the constitutionalisation of the Union. Consideration of the enumerated rights also highlights the exclusiveness of this status. The most important and significant of the rights are reserved for citizens, whereas those perceived to be less important are open to use by everybody. It should be remembered at this juncture that the rights attached to Union citizenship are to be found throughout the EC Treaty as per the wording of Article 8 (2) and are not limited to those specifically mentioned in Article 8.[24] Why did the drafters choose to emphasise certain rights? Some are new (for example the right to take part in local elections in a member state other than that of your nationality) but it is questionable whether the repetition of pre-existing rights in Article 8 adds anything to their value or scope.[25] If positive reasons for the enumeration may not be discovered (i.e. if there is no amelioration in the significance of these rights) then negative implications may be adduced and the selection of such rights seen as an attempt to delineate the boundaries of these relatively important rights (in the sense that they have tangible and very obvious benefits for people) by confining them to citizens only. If further developments of this nature are to be observed (in particular the association of human rights with citizenship) the indications are towards increasing élitism and social closure within the EU – Europe for (white) Europeans only.

It is in so significantly attaching economic rights to political ones that the problems have been created (as will be seen, the primary right attached to citizenship is free movement, essentially an economic right as that movement has traditionally been limited to persons in specified economic categories). The issue of whether political rights should be confined to nationals, so to speak, is not without problems,[26] but the justifications for the deprivation of economic rights are difficult to perceive when it is obviously of benefit to the EU market as a whole to allow maximum participation in goods and services markets.[27] The continued refusal to allow economic participation on nationality grounds may come to be regarded in the future as an embarrassing phase in European integration, when its obvious racist motivations and effects are fully appreciated.[28]

The free movement right

The affiliation of citizenship with the economic is made very clear in the specific rights to which Article 8 refers. Article 8a (1) lists as the first right of citizens the 'right to move and reside freely within the territory of the Member States ...'. On the most cursory of glances this seems to suggest a duplication of rights; free movement provisions have been enshrined in the EC Treaty since the establishment of the EEC in 1957. Have these provisions now seemingly been transformed into a constitutionally significant semi-political right? Articles 48–66 EC Treaty provide the basic provisions governing free movement of persons and services within the Community and as such constitute one of the fundamental freedoms of the E(E)C.[29] Though described as free movement of 'persons', the provisions are more limited and relate mainly to the free movement of economic actors; those who were seen as contributing to, and whose contribution was regarded as necessary for, the economic community – namely workers and self-employed persons.[30] As with many aspects of the EC Treaty, the ECJ has played a major role in what might generously be described as 'interpreting' these provisions. Thus, its jurisprudence has been responsible for confirming that only EC national workers may benefit from free movement. However, the Court has also extended the provisions of the Treaty to categories not specifically mentioned.[31]

Thus free movement rights prior to the introduction of EU citizenship covered most categories except non-nationals and residual non-economic actors such as children or gypsies. The association of free movement with citizenship does not make it clear whether this is an attempt to confine the rights in some manner or whether it is intended that they be expanded to cover persons not previously covered. Article 8a (1) reads 'subject to the limitations and conditions laid down in this Treaty'. If it is the case that this right is so subject, then it would appear that, even though identified as the primary element of citizenship, it is not available to all nationals of member states but only to those economically active. The *Adams* case[32] may well provide some answers from the ECJ on these issues. However, this analysis of Article 8 exposes its obvious inherent weaknesses. These defects may be the product of loose drafting, but if any real significance beyond the purely symbolic was intended in the invention of citizenship it ought perhaps to have merited more careful consideration.[33] If citizenship is to be regarded as a formal element of constitutionalisation of the Treaties it does not evidence any serious consideration on the part of the member states.

Can the same be said of the other rights granted under Article 8? Citizenship was loudly hailed as creating a direct political link between the people of Europe and the EC/EU.[34] How real is this claim? Article 8b asserts the right of citizens to vote and stand as a candidate in both European Parliament (Article 8b (2)) and local elections (Article 8b (1)) in member states in which they reside.[35] There is no doubt that these are innovatory rights. It might be asked, however, what connection there is between the Union and the right to vote in local elections?[36] The position of non-EC nationals is a further consideration in this regard; many will have been resident for many years in member states without having acquired the nationality of that state and are often therefore deprived of political rights, despite actively contributing to the economy of those states.[37] Thus Article 8b (1) creates a situation whereby long-term resident non-EC nationals have few or no political rights, but an EC citizen is able to exercise greater political rights based on a short period of residence. This creates and increases discrimination. With some consideration, rights of this nature could have been based on residence rather than nationality and seen as a positive contribution to an anti-racism statement on the part of the EU.[38]

As regards the EP election rights, it cannot be said to be insignificant that such rights are now available. However, they must be seen in the context of the role and powers of the European Parliament, both of which are relatively limited. There is a tendency to the notion that increasing EP powers and further connections between citizens and the Parliament will somehow solve the democratic deficit. This, of course, is not the case and it is disingenuous for the Commission to continue to propagate such notions. At any rate, the extent to which people vote in EP elections rather negates the view that they feel it to represent them or that it is the institution they identify with.[39]

Additional rights

The additional rights attached to citizenship are the right to diplomatic protection in a third country if their own state is not represented (Article 8c) and the rights to petition the European Parliament and to complain to the Ombudsman (Article 8d). These rights can only be seen as an attempt to pad out this section of the Treaty to give the impression of a healthy bundle of rights. Article 8c demonstrates a certain arrogance on the part of the EU, in that there may well be third states who will not recognise protection by another Member State and also a duplication, as this can hardly be described as a substantial right, given the widespread representation of EU states.

There is a certain archaically attractive sound to the petition right, reminiscent, as it were, of more monarchical type of government. But in reality the right will be familiar as it existed prior to the TEU – Article 138d EC. Interestingly, further reading of this article reveals that it is not confined to privileged EU citizens and also that it is limited to 'the Community's fields of activity'. So it is neither a new right, nor a citizenship right, nor does it relate to the Union as a whole. The right to complain to the Ombudsman 'concerning instances of maladministration in the activities of the Community institutions or bodies' is equally open to all residents in the EU. It does represent a Maastricht innovation but can hardly be said to advance the cause of democratic legitimacy.

Conclusion

That there would be a European Union citizenship was undoubtedly inconceivable even 10–15 years ago, let alone at the time of the formation of the Communities. Whether one regards this development as positive or otherwise depends upon one's position on the current state of European integration. It is ostensibly a step towards increased supra-nationality of the Union but its substance reflects little commitment on the part of the member states. If Article 8 is to remain no more than a symbolic statement then it insults the very people whom it proposes to benefit.

Citizenship and human rights will necessarily form part of any discussion of the constitutionalisation of the Treaties. Continued European integration rests upon a serious consideration of these matters, perhaps in a less heated and politically sensitive environment than that of the IGC negotiations.

Notes

1 This is a current buzz word in much EC/EU legal and political scholarship partly supported by developments at institutional level; the European Parliament has prepared a draft EU Constitution (EP 203.601, A3–003/94) and the Commission has endorsed a constitutional approach for the forthcoming Inter-governmental Conference. For recent discussion on the subject see Bellamy (1995) and Harden (1994), amongst others.
2 'The equality of political rights, which is the first mark of American citizenship, was proclaimed in the accepted absence of its absolute denial' (Shklar, 1991, p.1).
3 For longer discussions on citizenship generally see Brubaker (1992), Clarke (1994) and van Steenbergen (1994), amongst others.
4 Arguably, EU citizenship is so limited in nature that it is doubtful whether it merits classification as such.
5 *Piermont v France*, (March 1995), European Court of Human Rights case in which the Court partly based its decision upon the existence of

EU citizenship (case involving the deportation of a German national from French Polynesia).

6 If the number of people who voted in the 1994 European parliament elections in another member state is an indication of the level of awareness of the rights attached to EU citizenship, then it appears that it remains a relatively closely guarded secret (*European Commission – Rapport sur le Fonctionnement du TUE*, Brussels, 10 May 1995, Annex 1). The percentages vary from 32.29 per cent in Ireland to 1.57 per cent in Greece, with the average across the Community being approximately 10 per cent of those eligible having voted. These figures will have been affected by the degree to which 'host' member states publicised the availability of the right. Here, as in many aspects of EU citizenship, we see that effective exercise of rights is determined to some extent by member state discretion.

7 For details of the background to the introduction of EU Citizenship see Closa (1992), Kovar and Simon (1993), Meehan (1993a and b) and d'Oliveira (1994), amongst others.

8 It had been intended that there would be a direct link between citizenship and fundamental rights but this was not achieved and can be regarded as a major inadequacy (see further O'Leary, 1995). It could be argued, however, that an association between fundamental rights and citizenship would render the concept even more élitist in excluding fundamental rights protection from non-EU citizens in the field of EC law.

9 The question of whether EU citizenship can be regarded as declaratory or not was considered in the High Court in *R v. Secretary of State for the Home Department ex parte Gerard Adams*, 29 July 1994.

10 That is not to say that there had not already been non-economic developments in the EC; in particular the jurisprudence of the ECJ has been responsible in this regard. However, the functioning of the EC/EU remains fundamentally economically dictated.

11 Commission of the European Communities, *Report on the Citizenship of the Union*, COM (93) 702 adopted in accordance with the provisions of Article 8e, although because of delays in ratification of the TEU there was little to report on at that stage (December 1993). The Commission's Report on the Functioning of the TEU (effectively its first formal contribution to the 1996 IGC negotiations) contains a more in-depth and critical review of Article 8 and its implementation (see note 6 above).

12 *R v. Secretary of State for the Home Department ex parte G Adams*, High Court, 29 July 1994.

13 Citizenship-based arguments have also been raised in another case in the English courts – the *Phull* case – where the provisions of Article 8a have been invoked (in the High Court and the Court of Appeal) in order to prevent the deportation of the wife of a British citizen to India.

14 'The magic wand of dramatic language is waved in Article 8 (1) ... [it is] reminiscent of the first verses of the Gospel according to Saint John

[and] defies the incredulity of doubting Thomases who believe that "*ex nihilo nihil*" (d'Oliveira, 1994, p.131).

15 Nationals of only three member states – Denmark, France and Ireland – participated in referenda concerning the ratification of the TEU. One can easily identify figures in public life who would wish to disassociate themselves from the concept, let alone imagine the many millions of less public nationals who might object to this forcible linking with the EU.

16 One example is the right which states in the United States had to determine citizenship of individual states prior to the creation of federal citizenship under the Fourteenth Amendment to the Constitution. This practice resulted in citizenship criteria varying from state to state depending upon the state's needs. See Raskin (1993) for lengthy discussion of these issues.

17 Declaration No 2 '… the question whether an individual possesses the nationality of a Member State shall be settled solely by reference to the national law of the Member State concerned. Member States may declare, for information, who are to be considered their nationals for Community purposes by way of declaration …'. The second sentence implies that the discretion of the member states may operate so as to extend or reduce the category of nationals for Community purposes. See Closa (1995), O'Leary (1992) and d'Oliveira (1993) for further discussion of these issues.

18 The way in which member state discretion may be exercised in this context is demonstrated by two short examples: a high profile case in which UK citizenship was refused to Mohamed Al Fayed and Ali Fayed (resident in the UK for 30 years), allegedly because of their involvement in an anti-government scandal (*The Guardian* and *The Times*, 4 March 1995); and a recent Conseil d'Etat decision in France quashing a refusal to renaturalise long-time resident nationals of Mali and the Central African Republic because they were potentially polygamous and therefore unable to assimilate (see note of Errera, 1994, p.495). Future problems may be anticipated from the way in which potential EU states are developing their nationality laws and thereby excluding large minorities of long term residents – e.g. Latvia, where a recent Nationality Act has prevented many residents of ex-Soviet nationality from acquiring Latvian nationality.

19 Article 5 EC '[Member States] shall abstain from any measure which could jeopardise the attainment of the objectives of this Treaty'.

20 The UK 'opt-out' from the Social Protocol and Agreement under the TEU is an obvious example.

21 The European Parliament, in a Report on a Constitution for the EU (A3–0031/94 – 27 January 1994), implies in Article 47 of the Draft Constitution that member states which have not ratified the Constitution would have to choose to leave the Union.

22 This situation contrasts with other federal structures where it is not conceivable that a state would leave the federation and fundamental rights (political and social) are protec.ed by federal instruments.

23 It is almost certain that fundamental rights will be discussed at the 1996 IGC as several member states – including Spain, where the first meeting will be held in December 1995 – and the Commission and Parliament have raised these issues.

24 Although this raises problems in connection with the UK Social Protocol and Agreement 'opt out' as UK national EU Citizens cannot be said to have exact parity of status with other EU citizens.

25 Initially the Commission suggested that such rights are granted 'constitutional status' (see note 11 above) and the *Adams* ECJ reference may elucidate what this means. But it is not clear that duplicate references for some rights can alter their status. The Commission IGC Report (note 6 above) however, acknowledges that Article 8 enumeration does not improve the rights to any extent (p.8). This inconsistency does not aid in analysis of the implications of Article 8 and further highlights its weaknesses.

26 See Raskin (1993) for discussion of this issue in the United States.

27 The implications of excluding a potential 10–15 million long term resident non-nationals from the employment and service markets of the Union is, apart from its discriminatory consequences, arguably contrary to Articles 2 and 3 EC Treaty in its potential to distort competition within the EU (Hoogenboom, 1993). See generally Spencer (1994a and b).

28 See Hoogenboom (1993) and Groenendijk (1993), both of whom emphasise the fact that a group of second-class persons has been created by EC free movement provisions. The Commission has recently adopted a proposal for a Directive which extends limited free movement benefits to non-nationals.

29 For a longer discussion of free movement of persons in the EC see, for example, Steiner (1994).

30 There are many commentaries on the reasons why free movement rights came to be regarded as the privilege of specified sectors when arguably the original drafters may not have intended such limitations.

31 For example, receivers of services in the *Cowan* case – *Cowan v Tresor Public* (case 186/87) [1989] ECR 195 – a potentially crucial case as this category has the ability to encompass most persons who go to another member state, whatever their purpose. See O'Keeffe (1993) who suggests that *Cowan* may be used to justify extending free movement rights to non-nationals (p.520). However, in *Adams* the High Court rejected *Cowan* as a basis for allowing free movement to G. Adams. This appears to constitute an erroneous interpretation of *Cowan*.

32 See note 9 above.

33 The Commission IGC Report (note 6 above) acknowledges the weak nature of citizenship outlining its sporadic and incomplete rights.

34 See Commission Report on Citizenship, COM (93) 702.

35 Article 8b (1) was found to be incompatible with the French Constitution by the Conseil Constitutionnel and this was one of the reasons why a referendum was held in France before the ratification of the TEU. See Oliver (1994).

36 See d'Oliveira (1994, p.139). He also questions whether this right to vote is to be regarded as a right, or as a duty, as it is in some member states.

37 Citizenship may not have been acquired either because of restrictive *jus sanguis* nationality laws (such as in Germany) or perhaps because dual citizenship is not permitted by the nationality laws of the non-EC country they might be affiliated with (such as Turkey). Brubaker (1992, p.27) draws attention to this effective taxation without representation and observes; '[T]hat the exclusion of non-citizens from the franchise for national elections has nowhere been seriously challenged, even in the many European states with sizable populations of long-term resident non-citizens, testifies to the force – indeed the axiomatic status – of nationalism in modern states'.

38 The EC makes many public gestures towards tackling racism (such as at the Corfu European Council) but ignored the implications of citizenship and the opportunities it presented.

39 One might suggest that an input into the determination of the Commission President would be perceived by many as a more direct representation 'in Brussels', given the high profile of this post. The Commission IGC Report provided figures for the level of take up of the Article 8b (2) rights in the June 1994 EP elections: only one non-national candidate was elected out of a total of 57 who stood as candidates; see note 6 above for voting figures.

References

Bellamy, R., Buffachi, V. and Castiglione, D. (eds.) (1995), *Democracy and Constitutional Culture in the Union of Europe*, Lothian Foundation Press: London.

Blackburn, R. (ed.) (1993), *Rights of Citizenship*, Mansell: London.

Brubaker, R. (1992), *Citizenship and Nationhood in France and Germany*, Harvard University Press: Cambridge, Mass.

Clarke, P.B. (ed.) (1994), *Citizenship*, Pluto Press: London.

Closa, C. (1992), 'The concept of citizenship in the Treaty on European Union', *Common Market Law Review*, Vol. 29, pp.1137–69.

Closa, C. (1995), 'Citizenship of the Union and Nationality of the Member States', *Common Market Law Review*, Vol. 32, pp.487–518.

Durand, A. (1979), 'European Citizenship', *European Law Review*, Vol. 4, pp.3–14.

Errera, R. (1994), *Public Law*, Autumn, p.495.

Evans, A.C. (1984), 'European Citizenship: a novel concept in EEC Law', *American Journal of Comparative Law*, Vol. 32, pp.679–715.

Groenendijk, C.A. (1993), 'Three questions about Free Movement of Persons and Democracy in Europe' in Schermers, H. et al. (eds.) *Free Movement of Persons in Europe*, Martinus Nijhoff: Dortrecht.

Harden, I. (1994), 'The Constitution of the European Union', *Public Law*, pp.609–24.

Hoogenboom, T. (1993), 'Free Movement and Integration of non-EC nationals and the logic of the internal market' in Schermers et al. (eds.), op. cit.

Kovar, R. et Simon, D. (1993), 'La Citoyenneté Européenne', *Cahiers de Droit Européen*, Nos. 3–4, pp.285–316.

Meehan, E. (1993a), 'Citizenship and the European Community', *Political Quarterly*, Vol. 63, pp.172–86.

Meehan, E. (1993b), *Citizenship and the European Community*, Sage: London.

O'Keeffe, D. (1993), 'Comments on the free movement of various categories of persons' in Schermers et al. (eds.), op. cit.

O'Leary, S. (1992), 'Nationality law and community citizenship: a tale of two uneasy bedfellows', *Yearbook of European Law*, Vol. 12, pp.353–84.

O'Leary, S. (1995), 'The relationship between community citizenship and the protection of fundamental rights in community law', *Common Market Law Review*, Vol. 32, pp.519–42.

Oliver, P. (1994), 'The French Constitution and the Treaty of Maastricht', *International and Comparative Law Quarterly*, Vol. 43, pp.1–25.

d'Oliveira, H.U.J. (1994), 'European Citizenship: its meaning, its potential' in Dehousse, R., *Europe after Maastricht*, Law Books in Europe: Munich.

d'Oliveira, H.U.J. (1993), 'Commentary on case C–369/90, MV Micheletti v. Delgacion del Gobierno en Cantabria', *Common Market Law Review*, Vol. 30, pp.623–37.

Raskin, J.B. (1993), 'Legal aliens, local citizens: the historical, constitutional and theoretical meanings of alien suffrage', *University of Pennsylvania Law Review*, Vol. 141, pp.1391–470.

Shklar, J. (1991), *American Citizenship*, Harvard University Press: Cambridge, Mass.

Spencer, S. (ed.) (1994a), *Strangers and Citizens*, Trentham/IPPR: London.

Spencer, S. (ed.) (1994b), *Immigration as an economic asset*, Trentham/IPPR: London.

van Steenbergen, B. (ed.) (1994), *The Condition of Citizenship*, Sage: London.

Steiner, J. (1994), *EC Law*, Blackstone: London.

8 The communitarian ghost in the cosmopolitan machine: constitutionalism, democracy and the reconfiguration of politics in the New Europe[1]

Richard Bellamy and Dario Castiglione

Introduction

The end of the Cold War has unleashed forces likely to produce a dramatic reconfiguration of politics. Military competition powered the development of the nation state, providing the rationale for its monopoly of violence and its claims to territorial sovereignty. The states system now confronts both internal and external pressures that threaten to tear it apart.[2] On the one hand, the globalisation spawned by new technology stresses greater collaboration at an international level, particularly with regard to the economy, defence and environmental policy. On the other hand, the increased differentiation and complexity of social life that results from these developments has enhanced heterogeneity within states, fuelling a resurgence of ethnic and nationalist separatism and promoting multiculturalism. Though related, these two processes move in contradictory directions. The cosmopolitanism engendered by the first is undercut by the growing strength of communitarian sentiments and attachments fostered by the second. Reconciling these two trends raises fundamental issues concerning the purposes, character and coherence of the constitutions of modern states. In particular, it entails a reconsideration of the relationship of constitutions to state sovereignty, national self-determination and the democratic procedures and political cultures which sustain and are framed by them (Bellamy, Bufacchi and Castiglione, 1995, 'Introduction').

The liberal democratic nation states that emerged during the 19th century offered a particular understanding of how these elements related to each other. Nationalism provided the ideological glue that defined a relatively circumscribed group of people and unified them around a set of shared institutions and practices that were informed by a common political culture and were sovereign over a well-defined territory. Political community, loyalty, accountability and legitimacy were tied in this way to state power and authority (Habermas, 1992). Within this context, it became possible to present the constitution, be it written or unwritten, as expressing the on-going will of the people. Language, myths and history, more than any allegiance to a given set of principles, helped turn the constitution into a national symbol and part of a common heritage that expressed 'how we manage our affairs here'.

These constitutional settlements were never perfect by any means, as 19th and 20th century European constitutional history amply testifies. Consti-tutions themselves were often the object of disputes about whether they truly represented the spirit of the nation (Jaume, 1992), and in many cases discussions about them took second place to the process of national uni-fication and were therefore given relatively little consideration (Pombeni, 1992b). Moreover, their undeclared purpose was frequently to keep a check on the strong tendencies towards democratisation which were then emerging in politics and society. In recent decades these constitutional settlements have become even more unsatisfactory. In Eastern and Central Europe, the establishment of liberal democratic regimes on traditional western models has been challenged not only by the transition to a market economy and the rigours of global competition, but also by internal divi-sions due to ethnic and religious conflicts. In Western Europe, the transfer of political and economic decision-making to the European Union has been matched by increased demands for regional autonomy, with national parliaments caught uneasily in between (Wallace, 1994). As a consequence, many of the traditional concepts of constitutional democracy, such as sovereignty, citizenship and representation, which have depended for their coherence on the notion of individuals as equal members of a relatively homogeneous 'nation state', have been called into question (Habermas, 1992; MacCormick, 1995a). Who has the right to decide a given issue, let alone where, when and how they can make that decision, have become contested questions whose answers vary according to the topic under consideration. The relationship between national sovereignty as expressed in established constitutional arrangements and democratic accountability once again appears problematic (Bellamy, Bufacchi and Castiglione, 1995).

This chapter reviews the main approaches currently canvassed by liberal political philosophers as a response to this situation. The next section briefly outlines them and identifies two as particularly relevant: the communitarian liberal and the liberal communitarian. Subsequent sections then explore how other writers have employed these two ways of thinking in their analyses of the problems confronting constitutionalism in East and West Europe respectively. We shall conclude by advocating a variant of the second, liberal communitarian, approach.

Liberals and communitarians

Contemporary political philosophers of a liberal temper have responded to the challenges to traditional conceptions of politics described above in roughly one of three ways. Some adopt a cosmopolitan perspective that seeks to uphold certain abstract individual rights or principles of justice as universal, thereby providing the constitutional basis for all legitimate democratic regimes (e.g. Pogge, 1994). For these theorists, questions of national or cultural identity are of secondary importance, since our primary status is that of citizens of the world. Others argue from a more communitarian point of view. They generally stress that our individuality, and hence our rights, are social and cultural constructs and change according to context.[3] They think democracy should be privileged over constitutionalism because it allows the community to give expression to its own particular values (e.g. Walzer, 1981; Sandel, 1987). Increasingly, however, philosophers have become dissatisfied with drawing too sharp a distinction between liberal and communitarian positions and have attempted to mix the two approaches (e.g. Rawls, 1993; Taylor, 1989).[4] If the first champions the claims of the constitution and the second those of democracy, the third seeks a reworking of the two that aims to adapt the fusion between them achieved in the past by the nation state to the new social and political context of the present.

This mixed strategy has been developed in two different directions, with one placing more emphasis on the virtues of cosmopolitan-oriented constitutionalism and the other on communitarian-based defences of democracy. The first attempts to respond to communitarian-oriented criticisms of the kind of cosmopolitan approach which Rawls famously defended in *A Theory of Justice* (1971). This thesis may be defined as communitarian *liberal,* since it accepts the communitarian account of the embeddedness of the self and of morality within a given culture and set of traditions, but argues that in pluralist societies it remains important to reach common ground on a set of universal principles of justice by abstracting from these communally based identities. These principles serve as a constitutional foundation and precondition for politics of a non-metaphysical kind. Constitution-making is seen as part of a pre-commitment strategy aimed, on the one hand, at *limiting* politics, so as to protect pre- and extra-political spheres, and on the other hand, at *promoting* politics by entrenching democratic rights, functionally dividing power between various state agencies, devising mechanisms to minimise collective action problems and reducing the possible overloading of politics itself (Holmes, 1988). The crux of communitarian liberalism, as implicitly suggested by the 'new' Rawls of *Political Liberalism* (1994), is in anchoring the pre-commitment strategy within an overlapping consensus on a political conception of justice, so that this may on reflection offer a principled justification for the particular exclusions on which well-ordered constitutional regimes can be based.

The second interpretation of the mixed strategy can be defined as liberal *communitarian*. It is well illustrated by the dualist model of democracy advanced in Bruce Ackerman's *We the People* (1991). He claims (at least most of the time) that the democratic will as expressed during moments of 'constitutional' politics is the source of the liberal settlement that frames the 'normal' politics of self-interested citizens. During exceptional circumstances, politics is characterised by the genuine, protracted and public-spirited involvement of the majority of the citizenry. As a result, self-interest gives way to a concern with the common good that allows constitutional principles to emerge. In this way, politics proves both self-constituting and self-limiting, thereby resolving the notorious paradox of constitutionalism and democracy.

Although the versions of the mixed strategy outlined above refer principally to the experience of the United States, both models have been touted as solutions to the current crises of European politics. According to a number of commentators, the break up of traditional loyalties and established state structures in Europe now makes the new world an appropriate model for the old to follow. Habermas, for example, regards the American Constitution as a singular instance of a 'constitutional patriotism' that has successfully replaced the nationalist and ethnic ties of the immigrant population with an allegiance to certain common political values and principles. His call for the European Union to coalesce around an 'overlapping consensus of a common, supranational shared political culture' (Habermas, 1992, p.7) clearly echoes the communitarian liberal approach to the problem of pluralism.

In contrast, Ackerman (1992) has suggested that the events of 1989 provided a perfect opportunity for constitutional politics of a liberal com-munitarian type. He saw them as a favourable terrain for the prosecution of a 'liberal revolution' and the establishment of dualist forms of democracy in those countries. He has stressed the importance of involving the people in the framing of the new constitutions. He rejects the simple recourse to judges as founders, adopted by Germany in 1945. This strategy would prove both difficult, because the existing judiciary were too implicated with the old regime, and élitist, thus failing to engage the support of either the political class or the general populace in the resulting settlements.

In the remainder of this paper, we shall suggest that the complexity and plurality of modern societies make appeals to a primordial and abstract consensus hard to sustain. This problem is especially acute in countries engaged in a process of political transformation, as is the case in Central and Eastern Europe and, to a lesser extent, in the European Union. The communitarian liberal strategy proves inadequate, therefore. Rather than conceiving of constitutionalism as the mere exclusion of potentially divisive issues from politics, we argue that the restructuring of Europe requires a development and radicalisation of Ackerman's position. In particular, we wish to emphasise the *positive* aim of constructing democratic institutions that facilitate informed decision-making through the mediation and harnessing of conflicts and the political transformation of preferences. This step involves not just constitutional politics but also a political constitutionalism that employs the resources of politics as part of the constitutional framework. Such an approach treats constitutions as a form of government rather than as just a set of judicially protected legal norms.

Eastern Europe

It has recently been argued (in Offe, 1994, Ch. 4) that the political transformations occurring in Central and Eastern Europe differ greatly from the post-war 'modernisation' and democratisation processes studied in the specialised literature and often cited as examples for these countries to follow (O'Donnell, Schmitter and Whitehead, 1986). The experiences of the post-fascist regimes after 1945, of a number of Southern Mediterranean countries in the '70s and of the new democracies emerging in South America, are all instances where the establishment of new political and constitutional rules has, on the whole, occurred within already defined national and economic contexts. In contrast, the collapse of the socialist regimes of the former Eastern bloc has involved three separate transformative processes: namely, (1) the reconceptualisation of the boundaries and balance of power between states and of national and ethnic identities within single nation states; (2) the radical transformation of institutional structures, involving the redefinition of both sovereignties and the rules of the political game; and (3) the establishment of a new socio-economic system by the reintroduction of market competition and property and contractual rights, a development which has deeply affected the whole of the social structure of these societies and their internal distribution of power. The magnitude of these three crises has made the task of constitutional reform particularly demanding, posing dilemmas for both the communitarian liberal and the liberal communitarian approaches.

The communitarian liberals' suggestion that at the basis of a well-ordered constitutional regime there is an overlapping consensus on a political (in the sense of non-metaphysical) conception of justice may well apply to countries where such an overlapping consensus has already emerged, but its application to countries undergoing a process of democratic transformation places theory and practice in a vicious circle. In particular, commentators have observed that although the developments of democratic structures and constitutionalism are usually mutually supportive, democratic participation often obstructs economic change (Przeworski, 1991, pp.180–7; Elster, 1992, pp.15–7; Offe, 1994, pp.64–76). However, the economic reforms are considered to be a necessary requirement for the long-term stabilisation of constitutional democracy in these countries. As a result, a paradoxical tension between democratic and economic reform has emerged.[5]

Communitarian liberals insist that the circle must be broken at an ideal level by anchoring the history and tradition of a political community to universalistic meanings expressed in what Habermas (1992, p.7) has called the 'patriotism of the constitution'. But since neither this form of patriotism nor Rawls's 'overlapping consensus' are established overnight, they seem ultimately to rely on moral resources which are either not yet available or still scarce. It would appear that in order for a well-ordered constitutional democracy to be established and given stability, some more specific anchorage for the people's allegiance must be sought. In this gap, we submit, constitutional politics and its more sundry means play a fundamental role.

Nevertheless, difficulties exist for liberal communitarians as well. In many respects, Ackerman's hope that the new nations which arose from the collapse of communism would seize the constitutional moment has been dashed already. In almost every case, this strategy has been passed over in favour of other options. Instead of a liberal communitarianism involving political bargaining and arguing and which forces the critical appraisal of how individual and group values and interests relate to those of others, these countries have been characterised by the polarised pluralism that rests on an unreflective attachment to community or individualistic purposes.

Unwelcome though this situation is, its origins and drawbacks should not be misunderstood. It results neither, as some fear, from the over-politicisation which may have characterised constitution-making processes in these countries; nor from the half-hearted way in which constitutional arrangements have been made and sometimes unmade. The politicisation of constitutional debates in periods of dramatic change and heightened passions, particularly when the stakes are high, is not something which can be avoided, nor – in principle and within reasonable limits – something to be entirely discouraged. This is true particularly when conflict takes the form of genuine political confrontation, reflecting real and widespread interests and values within the polity, and when the scope for manipulation is limited and the imbalance of power only relative. Indeed, this kind of politicisation of constitutional moments follows from the very conception of 'constitutional politics' outlined by Ackerman.

As for the fragile and temporary nature of the constitutional settlements, this may not be an entirely negative thing either. In a situation of rapid political change, the tendency to settle for stop-gap constitutions is preferable to adopting bad constitutional charters that are then set in stone (Holmes, 1993). This caution applies not only to the basic rules and principles of the political system, which need the presence of an already developed network of political and pre-political organisations capable of representing the interests of the people in forms easily recognisable by and generally acceptable to them, but also to the entrenchment of fundamental rights and liberties. For the legitimacy of rights, although possibly not their philosophical justification, also requires democratic debate and endorsement (Bellamy, 1995).

Seeing entrenchment as part of an open-ended political process has two distinct advantages over the straightforward codification of certain putative universal principles. First, it allows the political definition – often over time – of a complex package of rights and duties establishing the balance between liberties and authority within a particular community. Such rights and duties are not simply directed to full members of the community itself, but also concern residents, non-citizens, unborn citizens and, indirectly, other communities and individuals. Second, it focuses on the need for institutions, practices, expectations and mental attitudes through which the entrenchment of rights can be given real content. From this perspective, for example, recent worries about the inclusion of social rights in the constitutional charters of Central and Eastern European countries prove unfounded (see Sunstein, 1992 and 1993 for the doubts and Schwartz, 1992 for a more optimistic view). Fears that the entrenchment of 'positive' rights in these nations risks fostering a dependency culture, thereby undermining both the introduction of a market economy and democratic constitutionalism at large, stem from seeing rights as a set of fixed, apolitical, abstract principles, whose definition and application involve no on-going contextualisation and no adjustment to particular histories and traditions.[6] In this respect, Ackerman's distinction between normal and constitutional politics is also too firmly drawn. They need to be combined in devising institutions that generate a consensus that previously did not exist – so that politics has to be seen as an intrinsic part of the constitution, rather than as occurring outside or within constitutional limits.

This analysis of the relative strengths and weaknesses of the proposals for Eastern Europe stemming, respectively, from communitarian liberals and liberal communitarians is borne out by a recent study by Claus Offe (1994). He contends that the East European experiment in social transformation requires a political economy of patience for its success (Offe, 1994, pp.76–80). This strategy rests on an unexpected consequence of economic progress which Albert Hirschman has called the 'tunnel effect' (Hirschman, 1981). Briefly, it appears that during periods of intense economic development and rising living standards, even people who are not direct and immediate beneficiaries of these improvements nonetheless maintain an attitude of goodwill towards the policies adopted and the system at large. This support largely stems from the hope factor and the assumption that an improvement in the lot of others provides a strong sign that one's own turn may soon come. For obvious reasons, however, the hope factor has a limited time span, which, as Hirschman notes, depends on the social structure of the society in question. Frustration, social discontent, disenchantment and unrest may follow should it appear to people that their expectations are unlikely to be fulfilled.

Hirschman compares the simple psychological mechanisms underlying this temporary tolerance of income inequality to the attitude of motorists trapped in a traffic jam in a tunnel, who draw hope from the fact that the cars in the lane next to theirs have started moving. Since the traffic jam is not of one's own making, but generally depends on factors external to the behaviour of the motorists themselves, everyone assumes that an improvement in the situation of others will eventually spread to them. However, if no advance occurs within a given time span, then those who are stuck in a queue begin to suspect foul play, a fact which is the source of acute irritation and eventually of reckless attempts to move into the next lane with results which may easily be imagined.

The application of the 'tunnel' metaphor to Central and Eastern Europe suggests that there are grounds for believing that people can and will trust the new democratic regimes whilst waiting for the economic reforms to work. Far from being a simple act of faith, such trust has a solid basis in mass psychology and normal expectations. Although the tunnel effect may work for a while, however, the trust it invokes will not last long unless two extra conditions are satisfied. First, it must be assumed that the 'projectual' capitalism[7] attempted in many of the Eastern and Central European countries can really deliver the goods of economic development and greater social welfare. This is partly an empirical question which does not concern us here, but is highly relevant to the second condition – namely, the careful management of the hope factor. Hope has to be extended sufficiently long for the reforms to prove themselves – or, in the event of failure, to give enough time for a different model of socio-economic organisation to be chosen with as little social disruption as possible.

Offe (1994, Chs. 4 and 5) suggests a number of ways in which the management of the hope factor might be facilitated. The first, almost trivial, way is the 'economic miracle' scenario. In this case, social patience can be left to manage itself. The second way can be assimilated into the communitarian liberal approach sketched earlier. It involves partially delegating to 'external' agents the devising of a mixture of incentives and sanctions that could act as a further motive to maintaining a democratic framework while economic forces are left to do their work. This option can be given political and constitutional substance by relying, for instance, on certain institutions of the international community (International Monetary Fund, European Community, etc.), on the charismatic role of certain leaders (a strong presidential system) or on a protected area for 'technical' decisions (an autonomous central bank, a powerful constitutional court, etc.),[8] so that they become the guarantors that today's sacrifices may not go unrewarded. The advisability of this approach depends on the amount of implicit trust it is feasible to ask people to place in the holders of such positions. However, besides relying heavily on paternalistic principles, this strategy may simply result in an overload of social patience.

The third way suggested by Offe is more promising and corresponds to a more liberal communitarian approach. This option associates the management of patience with the development of a series of virtues, institutions and techniques of social mediation. These can be considered under three main headings: civic virtue; civic associations; and social protection. The first may sound too much like the moral resources which the hope factor is meant to preserve while the situation gets better. Unfortunately, such virtue is rather fragile. Even if the motorists who observe the near line of cars moving possess a high degree of civility, there comes a point at which inaction in one's own lane will be strongly resented and 'uncivil' behaviour will follow. Offe, however, presents civic virtue not just as a set of civic principles and ethical attributes, but as the result of a moral infrastructure based on the techniques of self-observation and self-control which modern mass democracies have put in place and on the diffusion of autonomous and pluralist tastes (and criteria for judging tastes) fostered by complex modern societies.

The institutional aspect of civic virtue (what could be called the 'public sphere' of modern complex democracies) is very much linked to the second element of Offe's political economy of patience. This consists of the articulation within civil society of autonomous collective actors and associations. The protection and promotion of this space for collective action, organised according to heteronomous principles and pursuing autonomously chosen aims, is functional to the satisfaction of needs that are often independent of the level of economic development and income distribution. Consequently, patience is here fostered by multiplying the spheres of action where people can fulfil themselves and apply their own conception(s) of the good.

The third form of social mediation advocated by Offe involves the development of institutions and policies aimed at social and economic redistribution and protection. Within the context of the 'projectual' democratic capitalism described by Offe, the social state serves as a precondition for the establishment of a market economy in conditions of democratic politics, rather than being one of its possible products, as in the history of western capitalist societies. Whether or not the principles of the social state should be inscribed in the constitutions of the new states is, however, a matter of dispute, which depends on the balance between constitutional provisions and legislation and the procedures for constitutional revision. As we noted above, some commentators have argued that the constitutionalisation of positive rights is inappropriate in countries undergoing the transition from Communism to a market economy (e.g. Sunstein, 1992 and 1993). Not only are they regarded as unenforceable, thereby risking bringing the whole legal system into disrepute, they are also seen as hindering many of the reforms necessary to bring the new economic system into being. In particular, it is argued that their inclusion 'could work against the general current effort to diminish a sense of entitlement to state protection and to encourage individual initiative' (Sunstein, 1993, p.37). As such, they are luxuries that these countries can ill afford. Offe's analysis, in contrast, suggests that precisely the opposite may be the case. It may be the very presence of positive rights that gives individuals the hope and security to put up with the upheavals associated with the economic reforms and to risk engaging in entrepreneurial activities.

The social capital and moral resources that bind a society together take centuries to accumulate. Nevertheless, the political economy of patience here briefly outlined suggests that a start can be made through fostering forms and institutions of associational life that are capable of generating cooperative habits of reciprocity that moderate the pursuit of self or sectional advantage (see too Putnam, 1993, Ch. 6). A liberal communitarian strategy of devising institutions that promote constitutional politics, rather than the communitarian liberal advocacy of judicial frameworks that constrain it, are the main constitutional priorities, therefore.

The European Union

Parallel lessons can be drawn with regard to the European Union. The growing demand, during the 1980s, for the widening of the integration process beyond the scope of mainly economic orientated institution building culminated in the Maastricht Treaty and the stated aim of European Monetary Union. But the quickening of the pace of political unification that has resulted from these developments, together with the new responsibilities produced by the post-cold war situation, have raised fresh worries about the coherence and wisdom of the project.

Both doubts about and demands for greater political integration stem from reasonable concerns, reflected in the public opinion of each member country.[9] On the one hand, the fragmentation and ethnic and religious conflicts which have bedevilled the federal states of Central and Eastern Europe after the collapse of the communist regimes suggest some caution in attempting to superimpose a political community, based upon a largely fictional and vague supra-national identity, over well-established national allegiances (Shore, 1993; Wilterdink, 1993).[10] Many people, and not just unreconstructed nationalists and British Euro-sceptics, have started asking themselves whether a supra-national state in Europe will be able to guarantee democratic politics and standards of social civility in the way in which, on the whole, national states have done in the past. On the other hand, attempts at political and cultural integration are still half-hearted and lacking any clear vision. Habermas's concern that the absence of democratic control within the European Union may be more than a passing imbalance, reflecting instead the separation and complete autonomisation of the economic and the administrative systems from the rest of the life-world, should not be considered an entirely improbable scenario (see Habermas, 1992, pp.7–13; and, for similar worries from a constitutionalist's perspective, Zagrebelsky, 1994, 'Prefazione').

Opposition to and support for closer political ties originate respectively in either the fear or hope that the European Union is a polity in transition.[11] Both camps believe that the 'democratic deficit' needs addressing in one way or another. Some advocate stabilising the Union as a composite polity, with sovereignty firmly located at the national level. They regard its main function as the harmonisation of economic interrelations in view of growing market globalisation and competition. Others propose a federal Europe with new institutions and a radical reconfiguration of the political arena.

Resolving this debate between sceptics and federalists requires a more precise understanding of what the 'democratic deficit' really is. In its most general meaning, 'democratic deficit' is a deficit of both democratic representation and popular (substantive) legitimacy. This 'deficit' is the product of three 'incomplete' processes involving the building of: (1) political institutions (the democratic deficit, *strictu sensu*); (2) an internally coherent public law system (the constitutional deficit); and (3) inter- and intra-state institutions (the federal deficit) (see Duverger, 1991; Castiglione, 1995; and Zagrebelsky, 1994 respectively). Any consideration of the difficulties currently confronting the EU must address the various institutional and constitutional issues raised by all three of these 'deficits'. We shall suggest that the first two cannot be resolved without having already tackled the third.

A particularly useful approach to these issues can be found in the recent writings of Joseph Weiler (especially 1993, but see too 1991 and 1992). He distinguishes between formal and social or substantive legitimacy. Until recently, the formal legitimacy of the Union was not in question. The main treaties had the approval of national parliaments, whilst the European Court of Justice and the European Court of Human Rights ensure the procedural and, to some degree, substantive correctness of the decisions of the Commission, Council of Ministers and, where they touch on collective matters, member states. This formal legitimacy of Community institutions was taken to testify to the existence of a liberal communitarian style consensus between the various member states on the constitutional essentials of the Union as presently structured. However, Weiler remarks that European institutions still lack the broad degree of societal acceptance that makes for social legitimacy. We submit that only a liberal communitarian approach can promote this form of legitimation, and that without it there can be no way of bridging any of the three deficits identified above.

Weiler reasons that integration creates a democratic deficit in the first sense simply by virtue of enlarging the range of citizens to whom collectively binding decisions apply.[12] Formal legitimacy will not substitute for the resulting loss of control. Nor will improving the democratic accountability of centralised institutions – say, by increasing the powers of the European Parliament – necessarily resolve the issue. Such suggestions simply beg the question of the popular acceptability of community-wide decision-making, rather than offering a solution to the problem. Weiler (1993, p.257) remarks that 'in terms of social legitimacy no difference

121

exists between a decision taken in the Council of Ministers and a decision taken in the European Parliament' so that 'the single most legitimating element ... was the Luxembourg accord and the veto power'.

The 'constitutional' deficit has generally been viewed as the least troublesome of the three (Mancini, 1989). As we noted, the formal legitimacy of the Union largely rests on an acknowledgment of the legal validity of European treaties and bodies by the member states. However, the failure for such agreement to generate social legitimacy points to its limitations. Indeed, there are signs that in certain areas even this formal legitimacy of the Union is now being called into doubt. This possibility was highlighted by the recent judgment of the Constitutional Court of the Federal German Republic in response to the challenge by Mr Manfred Brunner and others to the validity of Germany's accession to the Maastricht Treaty.[13] Although this particular challenge failed, the Court chose to assert the continuing sovereignty of the German people and denied that either the European Court of Justice or any other European organ, either separately or corporately, could claim competence over its own competence. This competence-competence, so far as Germany was concerned, lay with the German Constitutional Court. A comparable view has also been expressed by the Conseil Constitutionnel in France. Here it was decided that derogations from the constitutional sovereignty of the French people could only be allowed if granted by a prior amendment of the Constitution that had been ratified by a referendum.[14]

These decisions suggest that the claim of European law to be treated as the 'higher law' of the Union is not as secure as many have assumed. Agreement on general norms, such as those embodied in the European Convention of Human Rights, does not obviate the desire of groups who feel tied by a special bond to interpret them for themselves (see Bellamy, 1995). Even when there is a deeper consensus on principles of justice than probably exists within the EU, differences over their practical implications will arise. Similarly, problems of incommensurability and non-compossibility amongst the basic liberties render authoritative procedures necessary to resolve the conflicts that result. As the German and French decisions cited above show, and the British objections to, and ultimate opt out from, the Social Chapter illustrate even more dramatically, in the absence of a high degree of substantive, social legitimacy for European institutions, the officials and populations of the member states will prefer such decisions to be taken domestically.

Continued assertions of sovereignty such as these would ultimately render the European project unworkable. If it is to survive, therefore, the European Union cannot count on formal legitimacy alone. Rather, means need to be found to promote a degree of identification with European institutions as competent decision-making bodies, at least in certain areas.[15] This largely entails tackling the federal deficit within the Union. A liberal communitarian approach, that draws on both constitutional politics and political constitutionalism, can play an important part in generating social legitimacy in this respect.16

So far, European institutions have been the work of economic and political élites, with significant decisions frequently being made behind closed doors, in 'rooms with no windows' (Chryssochoou, 1994; Wallace, 1993). As Albert Weale has remarked, the legitimacy theory underlying the integration process has considered popular support and identification mainly as the product of habit and successful (economic) performance. Consequently, there has been little consideration given to institutions, decision-making processes and procedures which aim to 'ensure that European governance is exercised in accordance with the consent of the governed' (Weale, 1994). No effort has been made to build a trans-national political movement for a democratic Community, and most parties and politicians remain centred on national politics.17 This fact has led a number of commentators to argue that democratic legitimacy within the Union can best be achieved by giving powers such as vetoes or a right to secede to nation states that guarantee their vital interests (Buchanan, 1990). Such measures assume that national communities have well-defined common interests, while it is only too apparent that processes of economic and technological globalisation produce both losers and winners within individual nation states. Moreover, they tend to encourage defection rather than engagement, thereby subverting rather than promoting the democratic process.

We believe that a far more positive approach is appropriate. Albert Weale (1995) has suggested that European institutions require a 'democratic baptism' in order to fashion a common identity and political vocabulary that recognises differences, yet affirms the need for mutual cooperation. Constitutional politics has the role not only of creating and legitimising shared political arrangements, but of creating a people by building a sense of commonality amongst the citizens of Europe (Ackerman, 1992; Castiglione, 1995). Nevertheless the credit gained from democratic baptism may soon begin to wane.

Political constitutionalism comes in here, reinforcing cooperative behaviour by encouraging a culture of compromise and accommodation in the bargained and argued settlement of conflict. Within such a system, political justice designates a *modus vivendi* achieved through a balance of power between interlocking democratic institutions, rather than an overlapping consensus on certain core constitutional values that may be upheld by a court of putative moral experts (Bellamy, 1995; Wincott, 1994). This scheme involves the creation of counter-balancing centres of decision-making that devolve power up or down to the most appropriate level in order to ensure that different values and interests get heard within the policy-making process. A distinction between normal and constitutional politics remains appropriate not because they reflect different qualities of decision-making but in order to differentiate between those decisions that are tied up with the practices and procedures of the whole system and those that reflect special contexts or on-going concerns. The former would need to be the preserve of a wider legislative body, such as a federal legislature, and might require special democratic protection, such as approval by a higher than average majority, or even, in cases of radical reform, the calling of a constitutional convention or a referendum. All of these are political mechanisms, however, that aim to secure the identification of citizens and governments with the norms that regulate their lives.[18]

Conclusion

Events in both East and West Europe pose a singular challenge to how we think about constitutionalism. A liberal cosmopolitan framework that simply relies on the judicial upholding of putative universal norms, proves too abstract to engage the allegiance of people when it comes to specific policy proposals. Similarly, a communitarian strategy that appeals to established traditions and conventions, underestimates the degree to which these have been eroded, often with good reason, by recent developments. As most philosophers now agree, some combination of the two now seems appropriate. We have suggested that a liberal communitarian strategy provides the best mixture in the current situation. The identification of the peoples of Europe with these new regimes can only be secured if constitutionalism is integrated with forms of democratic politics that give them a say in the framing and maintenance of the legal order governing their lives.

Notes

1   Research for this paper was supported by an ESRC research award for a project on 'Languages and Principles for a Constitution of Europe' (R000221170). We are grateful to audiences in Bologna, Bremen and Norwich for their comments on an earlier version. A companion piece to this chapter is forthcoming in the *British Journal of Political Science*.
2   See Hont (1994) for an overview of the formation and 'crisis' of the nation state as a driving political conception.
3   Charles Taylor (1989) has argued that there are two main issues – the ontological and the advocacy question – on which the communitarian-liberal divide can be drawn, and that these two questions should not be confused. In our context, this distinction does not really hold, since the advocacy position here analysed seems to be partly based on the ontological premise.
4   For a more sceptical view of the 'academic' debate between liberals and communitarians, see Zolo (1994).

5   Strictly speaking this is not presented as a logical paradox, since the experiences of western capitalist democracies are meant to have shown that it is possible to square the circle of democratisation and market-led economic development. But they have done so over time, and on the whole democratisation has followed economic development. The paradox applies to the countries in the process of transformation because they are asked to telescope the centuries-long emergence of democratic capitalism into a few years, in conditions of fierce economic competition, and to maintain democratic and constitutional regimes in the face of inevitable conflicts emerging from the internal redistribution of social and economic power.

6   On this point, see also next section.

7   I.e. the establishment of rules and institutions which have mainly grown out of the historical experience of western capitalism to societies which, particularly after almost 40 years of a statist socialist experiment, are not socially differentiated and lack an entrepreneurial social class.

8   Jon Elster and John Roemer have suggested this kind of heteronomous constitutionalism as the basis for a market socialism involving a separation between the control of the instruments of economic policy and that of the tools of social policy (Roemer and Elster, 1993, pp.38–9).

9   It is worth remembering that democracy was neither a requirement nor a priority in the European integration process (e.g. Mancini and Keeling, 1994).

10 For qualified defences of certain virtues of the nation states see Pocock (1991), Miller (1994) and the conversations between Ralf Dahrendorf, François Furet and Bronislaw Gemerek in Caracciolo (1992).

11 There is no logical reason why the present structure of the European Union could not last for a very long time and stabilise itself in the present form. This is ultimately the hope of the Euro-sceptics of many countries, although they fail to recognise how much sovereignty has already been displaced from its traditional national loci. Professor MacCormick has suggested to us in conversation that the present state of the Union could be described as a 'mixed polity'.

12 Weiler's formulation is, however, ambiguous. Strictly speaking, this is not a question of 'democratic deficit', but a variation on the well-known problem of the appropriate *dimensions* for a democratic polity, so that the enlargement of a community run according to democratic procedures does not result in a loss of democracy, but in a loss of control from the individual member's perspective. However, such loss of control may, as Weiler seems rightly to imply, become a question of democracy.

13 Ruling pronounced by the Federal Constitutional Court, Second Division, on 12 October 1993, 2BvR 2134/92, 2BvR 2159/92. For a useful discussion, see MacCormick (1995b).

14 92–308 DC, cited in MacCormick (1995b, p.256). Ironically, in view of Britain's reputation as the most Europhobic of the member states, the much vaunted doctrine of parliamentary sovereignty, which effectively hands constitution-making power to the executive, has meant that no such challenge has occurred here. On the contrary, the House of Lords decision in the *Factortame* case conceded that in acceding to the Treaty of Admission Britain had effectively derogated from its own future sovereignty until such time as Parliament decided to withdraw from the Union (*R. v Secretary of State for Transport ex. p. Factortame* [1991] AC 603; [1991] 3 All ER 769; C221/89, cited in MacCormick, 1995b, p.256).

15 See Abélès (1994), although he seems only to take into consideration the role of the European Parliament in such a new public sphere. On the role of public opinion in the process of European integration, and on how the public perception of the legitimacy of the Union as a policy-making centre varies from issue to issue, see Sinnott (1994).

16 Arguably the establishment of European Citizenship in Article 8 of the Treaty of European Union marks the start of official recognition of the legitimation issue and is an attempt to address it. However, as Carole Lyons' chapter in this volume shows, the Maastricht Citizenship Chapter offers little that is new and in many respects highlights the problem rather than resolving it.

17 In this respect, not enough attention seems to have been given to the feasibility of a European party-system, or to whether processes of globalisation and the emergence of *anti-political* feelings and forms of organisations within a number of European nations prefigure a change in the institutional role of political parties. Similar questions can be raised on the role of social movements within the European political and institutional context – see Tarrow (1994).

18 Several points of practical agreement might be possible between the position here advocated and the kind of 'institutional cosmopolitanism' recently described by Thomas Pogge, in so far as his scheme claims to be 'compatible with political units whose membership is homogeneous with respect to some partly unchosen criteria ... and it would certainly engender such units' (Pogge, 1994, p.115). A similar position, based on an expanded framework of democratic institutions crossing traditional boundaries, is also defended by David Held (1992).

References

Abélès, M. (1994), 'A la recherche d'un espace public Communautaire', *Pouvoirs. Revue Français d'études Constitutionnelles et Politiques*, Vol. 69, pp.117–28.

Ackerman, B. (1991), *We The People: Foundations*, Vol. I, Harvard University Press: Cambridge, Mass.

Ackerman, B. (1992), *The Future of Liberal Revolution*, Yale University Press: New Haven and London.

Bellamy, R., Bufacchi, V. and Castiglione, D. (eds.) (1995), *Democracy and Constitutional Culture in the Union of Europe*, Lothian Foundation Press: London.

Bellamy, R. (1995), 'The Constitution of Europe: Rights or Democracy?', in Bellamy, Bufacchi and Castiglione (eds.), ibid.

Caracciolo, L. (ed.) (1992), *La democrazia in Europa*, Laterza: Bari.

Buchanan, J.M. (1990), 'Europe's Constitutional Opportunity', in *Europe's Constitutional Future*, Institute of Economic Affairs: London.

Castiglione, D. (1995), 'Contracts and Constitutions' in Bellamy, Bufacchi and Castiglione (eds.), op. cit.

Chryssochoou, D.N. (1994), 'Democracy and Symbiosis in the European Union: Towards a Confederal Consociation?', *West European Politics*, Vol. 17, No. 4, pp.1–14.

Dunn, J. (ed.) (1994), 'Contemporary Crisis of the Nation State?', *Political Studies*, Special Issue, 42.

Duverger, M. (1991), 'L'Europe: balkanisée, communautaire ou dominé?', *Pouvoirs. Revue Française d'études Constitutionnelles et Politiques*, 57, pp.129–42.

Elster, J. (1992), 'Making Sense of Constitution Making', *East European Constitutional Review*, Vol. 1, No. 1, pp.15–7.

Habermas, J. (1992), 'Citizenship and National Identity: Some Reflections on the Future of Europe', *Praxis International*, Vol. 12, No. 1, pp.1–19.

Held, D. (1992), 'Democracy: From City-States to a Cosmopolitan Order?', *Political Studies*, Special Issue, 40, pp.10–39.

Hirschman, A.O. (1981), 'The Changing Tolerance for Income Inequality in the Course of Economic Development' in *Essays in Trespassing. Economics to Politics and Beyond*, Cambridge University Press: Cambridge.

Holmes, S. (1988), 'Precommitment and the Paradox of Democracy' in Elster, J. and Slagstad, R. (eds.), *Constitutionalism and Democracy*, Cambridge University Press: Cambridge.

Holmes, S. (1993), 'Back to the Drawing Board', *East European Constitutional Review*, Vol. 2, No. 1, pp.21–5.

Hont, I. (1994), 'The Permanent Crisis of a Divided Mankind: "Contemporary Crisis of the Nation State" in Historical Perspective' in Dunn (ed.), op. cit.

Jaume, L. (1992), 'Il potere costituente in Francia dal 1789 a De Gaulle' in Pombeni, P. (ed.), *Potere costituente e riforme costituzionali*, Il Mulino: Bologna.

127

O'Donnell, G., Schmitter, P. and Whitehead L. (eds.) (1986), *Transitions from Authoritarian Rule: Latin American and Southern Europe*, The John Hopkins University Press: Baltimore, 5 vols.

MacCormick, N. (1995a), 'Sovereignty, Democracy and Subsidiarity' in Bellamy, Bufacchi and Castiglione (eds.), op. cit.

MacCormick, N. (1995b), 'The Maastricht-Urteil: Sovereignty Now', *European Law Journal*, Vol. 1, No. 3, pp.255–62.

Mancini, G.F. (1989), 'The Making of a Constitution for Europe', *Common Market Law Review*, 26, pp.595–614.

Mancini, G.F. and Keeling, D.T. (1994), 'Democracy and the European Court of Justice', *The Modern Law Review*, Vol. 57, No. 2, pp.175–90.

Miller, D. (1994), 'The Nation-State: a Modest Defence' in Brown, C. (ed.), *Political Restructuring in Europe*, Routledge: London and New York.

Offe, C. (1994), *Der Tunnel am Ende des Lichts*, Campus Verlag: Frankfurt and New York.

Pocock, J.G.A. (1991), 'Deconstructing Europe', *London Review of Books*, 19 December, pp.6–10.

Pogge, T. (1994), 'Cosmopolitanism and Sovereignty' in Brown, C. (ed.), *Political Restructuring In Europe*, Routledge: London and New York.

Pombeni, P. (ed.) (1992a), *Potere costituente e riforme costituzionali*, Il Mulino: Bologna.

Pombeni, P. (1992b), 'Potere costituente e riforme costituzionali. Note storiche sul caso italiano 1848–1948' in Pombeni (ed.), op. cit.

Przeworski, A. (1991), *Democracy and the Market*, Cambridge University Press: Cambridge.

Putnam, R. (1993), *Making Democracy Work: Civic Traditions in Modern Italy*, Princeton University Press: Princeton.

Rawls, J. (1971), *A Theory of Justice*, Harvard University Press: Harvard, Mass.

Rawls, J. (1993), *Political Liberalism*, Columbia University Press: New York.

Roemer, J. and Elster, J. (1993), 'A Third Way?', *East European Constitutional Review*, Vol. 2, No. 1, pp.38–9.

Sandel, M. (1987), 'The Political Theory of the Procedural Republic' in Bryner, G. and Reynolds, N. (eds.), *Constitutionalism and Rights*, Brigham Young University Press: Provo, Utah.

Schwartz, H. (1992), 'In Defence of Aiming High', *East European Constitutional Review*, Vol. 1, No. 3, pp.25–9.

Shore, C. (1993), 'Inventing the "People's Europe": Critical Approaches to European Community "Cultural Policy"', *Man. The Journal of the Royal Anthropological Institute*, Vol. XXVIII, No. 4, pp.779–800.

Sinnott, R. (1994), 'Integration Theory, Subsidiarity and the Internationalisation of Issues: The Implications for Legitimacy', European University Institute, Florence, Working Paper, RSC No. 94/13.

Sunstein, C. (1992), 'Something Old, Something New', *East European Constitutional Review*, Vol. 1, No. 1, pp.18–21.

Sunstein, C. (1993), 'Against Positive Rights', *East European Constitutional Review*, Vol. 2, No. 1, pp.35–8.

Tarrow, S. (1994), 'Social Movements in Europe: Movement Society or Europeanization of Conflict?', European University Institute, Florence, Working Paper, RSC No. 94/8.

Taylor, C. (1989), 'Cross-Purposes: The Liberal-Communitarian Debate' in Rosenblum, N. (ed.), *Liberalism and the Moral Life*, Harvard University Press: Cambridge, Mass. and London.

Wallace, H. (1993), 'European Governance in Turbulent Times', *Journal of Common Market Studies*, Vol. 31, No. 3, pp.293–303.

Wallace, W. (1994), 'Rescue or Retreat? The Nation State in Western Europe, 1945–93' in Dunn, op. cit.

Walzer, M. (1981), 'Philosophy and Democracy', *Political Theory*, 9, pp.379–99.

Weale, A. (1994), 'Single Market, European Integration and Political Legitimacy', Paper presented at the 'Evolution of Rules for a Single European Market' ESRC conference, University of Exeter, 8–11 September, p.18.

Weale, A. (1995), 'Democratic Legitimacy and the Constitution of Europe' in Bellamy, Bufacchi and Castiglione (eds.), op. cit.

Weiler, J.H.H. (1991), 'The Transformation of Europe', *The Yale Law Journal*, Vol. 100, No. 8, pp.2403–83.

Weiler, J.H.H. (1992), 'After-Maastricht: Community Legitimacy in Post-1992 Europe', in Adams, W.J. (ed.), *Singular Europe: Economy and Polity of the European Community after 1992*, University of Michigan Press: Ann Arbor.

Weiler, J.H.H. (1993), 'Parliamentary Democracy in Europe 1992: Tentative Questions and Answers' in Greenberg, D. et al. (eds.), *Constitutionalism and Democracy. Transitions in the Contemporary World*, Oxford University Press: New York and Oxford.

Wilterdink, N. (1993), 'The European Ideal. An Examination of European and National Identity', *Archives Européennes de Sociologie*, Vol. XXXIV, No. 1, pp.119–36.

Wincott, D. (1994), 'Human Rights, Democracy and the Role of the Court of Justice in European Integration', *Democratization*, Vol. 1, No. 2, pp.251–71.

Zagrebelsky, G. (ed.) (1994), *Il Federalismo e la democrazia in Europa*, La Nuova Italia Scientifica: Roma.

Zolo, D. (1994), 'Prefazione', to id. (ed.) *La Cittadinanza. Appartenenza, identità, diritti*, Laterza: Roma-Bari.

Section Four
CONSTITUTIONALISM BEYOND THE SOVEREIGN STATE

9   A right to secede? Scotland reviewed

Elspeth Attwooll

Those of us who have signed the 1988 *A Claim of Right for Scotland* have committed ourselves to the view that the people of Scotland have a right to self-determination. The purpose of what follows is to explore what might be meant by such a right[1] and whether it does or should include a right to secede.[2] The first part of the discussion is concerned with analysing the extent to which such or similar rights are actually afforded by conventional rules, whether of law or 'positive political morality', and with assessing how far Scotland might benefit from them. The second part turns to arguments about whether (and if so, when) a right to secession should exist, again looking to how Scotland might fare if these arguments were persuasive ones. The final part suggests that the resolution of problems about secession depends on an adequate articulation of the basis of the wider right to self-determination and indicates what this sort of argument might involve.

Conventional rules

International Law

A right to self-determination is to be found in, for example: the UN Charter;[3] General Assembly Resolution 1514 (XV) of 1960;[4] the 1966 International Covenants on Human Rights; and the 1970 Declaration on Friendly Relations. Its beneficiaries are entitled 'freely to determine ... their political status and to pursue their economic, social and cultural development'. There are, however, difficulties in determining to whom exactly the right belongs. Although the beneficiaries are identified as 'peoples', what counts as a people is itself a contentious matter. Further, does the right extend to any group that may be designated 'a people' or only to those 'peoples' who find themselves in certain special sets of circumstances – for example,[5] those:

i) who have come under the rule of a state located at a distance from them – a so-called 'salt water' colonisation; and/or

ii) who have been conjoined with a neighbouring people in the course of a colonisation of the above kind – colonial encirclement; and/or

iii) who have been incorporated into a state when it has expanded by taking over adjoining territory – colonial annexation; and/or

iv) who, whether a majority or minority group within a state, have become the subject of oppression; and/or

v) who, within a democratic state, have aspirations to a level of autonomy which that membership is failing to satisfy?[6]

Before considering more fully arguments as to just who does benefit from the right, it seems appropriate to ask where amongst the above Scotland might be said to fit. (For this part of the argument, it is taken as a given that the Scots can be identified as a people.) The geography of Great Britain precludes the case of salt water colonisation and the lack of involvement of any external power that of colonial encirclement. This leaves only colonial annexation, subjection to oppression and aspiration to autonomy as possibilities.

In assessing the first, a little needs to be said about the nature of colonisation. Generalisation is difficult here, since much depends on the style of the coloniser, but it is suggested that colonisation involves: the taking over of territory, usually against the wishes of the existing population and with some, at least, use of force; the movement of varying numbers of the inhabitants of the colonising state into the territory, with these people controlling its administration and, very often, the exploitation of its natural resources; the imposition, again in varying degrees, of the cultural norms of the colonisers on the original population; and the removal of control by that population over its affairs. This process of domination may be such as to allow no self-government at all, or only on a very limited local basis, or at a more general level, but in any case only within the confines permitted by the coloniser[7] or through direct representation in the institutions of the coloniser.[8]

On this basis, are the Scots then:

A people colonised by annexation? Scotland and England were linked – if not in an altogether trouble-free fashion – by the succession of James VI of Scotland to the English throne in 1603. The unification of the two kingdoms in 1707 was as the result of a Treaty and of Acts of Union by the separate Parliaments. England secured her 'back door' and Scotland achieved free trade with her. The measure was not popular with the majority of Scots, many seeing it as the barter of Scotland for financial gain. Yet the union was brought about by the accepted constitutional authority of the time, and separate systems of church, education and law were guaranteed under it.

Arguably, then, what took place was not a colonisation but a voluntary merger. This might be taken to bar any right to secede, for, in 1972, the International Commission of Jurists adopted what they considered to be a widely held view amongst international lawyers that:

> if a people or their representatives have once chosen to join with others within a unitary or federal state, that choice is the final exercise of their right to self-determination; they cannot afterwards claim the right to secede under the principle of the right to self-determination (Secretariat, 1972, p.69).

They do, though, soften this somewhat by arguing that it is subject to the government's complying with the principle of equal rights and representing the people without distinction, so that, if one of the constituent peoples is discriminated against, their full right to self-determination revives.

Nonetheless, the basis of this 'single opportunity' approach is a doubtful one[9] and as soon as any exception is made, the whole issue of the grounds for self-determination is again opened up. Further, although the point cannot be fully justified here, it can be claimed that many of the effects of the merger under consideration have resembled those of a colonisation. In particular, since Scottish representation in the Westminster Parliament is very much in the minority, the opportunity for Scots freely to 'pursue their economic, social and cultural development' is at best a limited one. The situation is exacerbated at present by the extent to which the political complexion of its representation, as of Scotland as a whole, differs from that of England.

Clearly, though, the case from colonial annexation is, at best a slight one. So it may be asked, instead, are the Scots:

A people subjected to oppression? Identifying simply, if crudely, 'the Scottish people' with the population of Scotland,[10] there is no doubt that this population is a minority one, amounting to roughly one-tenth of that of Britain as a whole. To claim that this minority is subjected to oppression, however, might seem insulting to the many groups throughout the world whose members are or have been subjected to grave abuses of their human rights simply because of their membership of that group. There is, too, a paradox which arises out of the relatively secure existence of separate Scottish systems of church, education and law. These help to motivate the call for self-determination and would undoubtedly weigh considerably in any objective assessment of 'fitness' for it. At the same time, their very existence militates against regarding the Scots as being subject to alien oppression.

Nonetheless, oppression is arguably relative, in the degree that the burdens of arrangements outweigh their benefits. There is no doubt that many Scots do perceive themselves as, at least mildly, oppressed in this fashion. Whether this perception is a well-founded one is a matter of dispute. For example, the present government claims that the Scots are, economically speaking, net beneficiaries of the union. On the other hand, there is considerable evidence, both historical and contemporary, of the erosion of the distinctiveness of Scots institutions and, particularly recently, of reforms fitting ill with them.

If, then, the Scots are – at best or at worst – only very mildly oppressed, can they then be categorised as:

A people aspiring to a greater degree of autonomy than allowed for by a democratic polity? Much turns here on notions of democracy. If the presence of a right to democratic participation is taken to be the sole requirement for the existence of a democratic polity, and if all that this right requires is that everyone has a vote,[11] with the majority view prevailing, then the Scots do indeed belong to such a polity. Once one goes beyond this understanding, however, and starts asking questions about the effectiveness of that participation, the issue becomes rather less clear-cut. This is even more the case once it is suggested that the right to democratic participation is not the only kind of right that a democratic polity demands. The main point, however, in showing that the Scots do not belong to such a polity would be to reinforce a claim of subjection to oppression and, thus, to qualifying for self-determination on that basis.

If, on the other hand, a democratic polity is taken to exist, the question becomes simply one of whether the Scots do aspire to greater autonomy than membership of that polity currently allows. Here the evidence is clear. Both in terms of opinion polls in which the question is directly asked and in terms of the policies of the parties predominantly voted for, the answer is that approximately 75 per cent of them do so aspire. What is rather less clear is the kind of autonomy looked for. With some (about 25–30 per cent) it is independence, albeit, for most, within the European Union; with the remainder it is a matter of greater legislative control over internal affairs.[12]

In conclusion, then, one may argue that the people of Scotland are, at worst, in a quasi-colonial situation and subject to a very mild degree of oppression. Thus, they might qualify if the right of self-determination is afforded in such cases. Only if it extends to the aspirational situation, however, does their claim to be a beneficiary of the right seem to be a strong one.

Unfortunately, international law is of doubtful assistance here. Although Resolution 1541 (the 1960 Declaration) refers to 'All peoples', it was made in the context of de-colonisation and places its main emphasis on the removal of barriers to independence for dependent peoples. Further, in Article 6 it expressly states that '[a]ny attempt at the partial or total disruption of the national unity and the territorial integrity of a country is incompatible with the Purposes and Principles of the Charter of the United Nations'. The justification for this clause seems to be that such attempts would be a threat to international peace and security, the maintaining of which is stated as the first – and often regarded as the primary – purpose of the UN.

Although there has been some recognition, through General Assembly resolutions, of the existence of the right in other cases,[13] it is not clear what, beyond political rhetoric, is implied by these decisions – other, perhaps, than the articulation of grounds for the *ex post facto* legitimation of any successful measures of self-help. In particular, there is a wariness about according a right to self-determination to peoples within the boundaries of existing states, since this might be taken to imply a right to secede.

The dangers they believe consequential upon the existence of such a right have led some commentators to make a sharp distinction between colonial cases and intra-state ones,[14] on the basis that, with the former, there was no shared territory involved. One writer even asserts that '[f]or the purposes of self-determination under international law, peoples are to be defined by the populations of states, while different ethnicities in their territories constitute minorities' (Müllerson, 1994, p.91). Thus, the right to self-determination becomes simply that to participation in the democratic process.[15] If international law has a role, it is merely that of ensuring that this right is accorded to members of such minorities. This approach, though, appears dubious in a number of respects, not least in its attempt to solve the problem by definitional fiat.[16]

One may also question the consistency of the distinction being drawn between salt water colonial and intra-state situations. First, only the principle of the territorial integrity of existing states stands between salt water colonisations and cases where a state has encroached upon adjoining, already populated, territory. The effects on that population may differ little, if at all. Second, while many undoubtedly were oppressed, it is by no means clear that *all* previously colonised peoples were, if by this is meant subjected to an abuse of their human rights, or excluded from participation in the democratic process. In which case, their right to self-determination appears to have been generated either on the back of real cases of oppression or as a matter of expediency – because of a perceived threat to international peace and security – or as the result of some objection to colonisation *per se*. Yet, if this objection has any more than an emotional grounding, it is unclear on what principle it rests – unless, that is, an incapacity on the part of such groups and individuals freely to 'determine their political status and ... pursue their economic, social and cultural development' is, of itself, to be seen as an abuse of human rights or an effective exclusion from democratic participation. Yet, if that is so, it becomes difficult to see why this incapacity is any less abusive or exclusive in the case of peoples within territorial states. In consequence, it becomes necessary either to provide good reasons why the principle of territorial integrity should always be given priority or, alternatively, to admit of – a perhaps limited – right of secession.17

In conclusion, there is clearly not, at present, any explicit right in international law to which a Scottish bid to secede could appeal. Beyond this there is a clear division between those who would deny and those who would maintain that such a right is already implicit in the norms of international law as properly conceived.

It may be, however, that there is no need for Scots who wish to pray international law in aid to rely on the second of the two views prevailing. The United Kingdom of Great Britain was established by the Treaty and Acts of Union. If the Treaty actually provided for secession, then, since one of the fundamental principles of international law is *pacta sunt servanda*, any right so established would require to be honoured.

Domestic Law

At first sight, matters do not seem too promising. Article I of the Scottish Act reads:

> That the Two Kingdoms of Scotland and England shall, upon the first day of May next ensuing the date hereof, and forever after, be United into One Kingdom by the name of GREAT BRITAIN ...

What is less clear, however, is the effect of the union on the constitutions of the two kingdoms concerned, especially with regard to Article III, which stated: '[t]hat the United Kingdom of Great Britain be represented by one and the same Parliament to be stiled the Parliament of Great Britain'.

Five different understandings, at least, can be identified (for a full discussion of the issues see Upton, 1989). First, the pre-existing Scottish Constitution was abolished, while that of England remained intact, except for the admission of Scots to minority representation in the English Parliament. Second, both pre-existing constitutions were abolished and a new unitary one formed, with no restrictions on the new unitary Parliament. Third, while both pre-existing constitutions were abolished, the new unitary Parliament was restricted by the terms of the Treaty, if not the Acts, through which it was established. Fourth, both pre-existing constitutions were amended to the extent of uniting the kingdoms into one state – but of a federal or quasi-federal kind – with a Parliament that was to act variously as a United Kingdom, Scottish, and English and Welsh one, as occasion demanded. Fifth, both pre-existing constitutions were amended to the extent of uniting the kingdoms into one state, but of a confederal kind, with the Scottish and English Parliaments merely delegating their powers to the new one, which would act on their behalf, sometimes separately and sometimes simultaneously.

The problem comes in deciding which of these understandings is the most persuasive. If one looks to the intentions of the Scots negotiators and to most of the actual wording of the documents, then the third (or restricted Parliament) and the fourth (or quasi-federal) interpretations appear the most plausible. It is, though, far from clear that the intentions of the English matched those of the Scots.

Further, if we seek guidance from subsequent political and legal developments, then there is evidence to be found which supports most of the possibilities canvassed. On the one hand, there were a number of breaches in the spirit, if not the letter, of the arrangement almost from the moment it came into effect.18 On the other hand, we find Bentham (1967, p.100, n.1) suggesting, in 1776, that any alteration concerning the Act [sic] of Union, if it had been stipulated in favour of Scotland, should be invalidated if adequately petitioned against from within Scotland, even though only 'for the sake of preserving the public faith, and to avoid irritation to the body of the nation'. Other, and more recent, evidence points in various directions. One might, for example, cite both the separate treatment afforded to Scottish legislation and the tendency of the House of Lords, sitting as an appeal court, to fail to distinguish its Scottish and English roles.19

How, then, does all this bear on the existence of a right to secede? First, as it is domestic law that is under consideration, one might draw parallels with the law of divorce and the law of contract. Although the law of Scotland and England differs in some respects on this issue, the grounds for divorce in the United Kingdom currently centre on the irretrievable breakdown of the marriage, which, in certain circumstances, need only have occurred from the point of view of one of the partners. In Scotland, at least, all that is then required is appropriate proof, together with similar proof that suitable arrangements have been made for any children and that matrimonial property has been fairly apportioned. On this kind of parallel, then, one might argue that a domestic right to secede should require only specification of the appropriate proof: that the breakdown is irretrievable; that responsibilities to other, particularly dependent, entities will be met; that there is equity in the distribution of assets; and, possibly, that some short-term financial compensation will be given where one party is in need.

Drawing such a parallel is, however, controversial. In criticising the approaches of Buchanan (1991) and Nielsen (1993), R.E. Ewin (1994) argues that regarding secession as 'a political divorce' fails to distinguish between what it is to be a person and what it is to be a people. The gist of his argument is that it is government which constitutes a people and that without corruption or inadequacy in the prevailing government 'a multitude of persons will not be the sort of item that *could* secede' (Ewin, 1994, p.230). As will become clear later in the discussion, Ewin's analysis is itself a controversial one.[20] Nonetheless, it does draw attention to the fact that secession is a matter of the rights of groups rather than of individuals and that parallels with divorce should accordingly be approached with caution.

However, the law of contract is applicable to both categories. It is possible, though, to consider here only a few respects in which its principles might apply in relation to secession: the roles of *consensus*; of unreasonableness; and the consequences of breach. As to the first, it seems at least doubtful that there was, at the time of the Union, any genuine 'meeting of the minds' with regard to the meaning to be placed on the terms of the Treaty. It would seem likely, though, that any consideration of original *consensus* would be regarded as vitiated through time or by a doctrine akin to that of personal bar. With regard both to unreasonableness and breach, much turns on the interpretation put on the events of 1707 and on subsequent developments. As to unreasonableness, whilst Scots law did once make some concession to the view that a party was only entitled to perform a contract in a reasonable way, this approach was subsequently rejected by the House of Lords.[21] Nor does there seem much prospect of using something like the French doctrine of *imprévision* in administrative law, despite the point made by the Claim of Right that 'the spirit [of the Treaty of Union] has never affected the huge areas of government which have evolved since'.

In the area of breach of contract, there is room for disagreement as to the extent, if any, to which the provisions of the Treaty and Acts of Union have been violated and, thus, as to whether rescission is justified. One particularly interesting point arises, however, should Scotland, by rescinding without showing justification, become the actual author of the breach. For, when it comes to remedies, Scots law is reluctant to interdict people from omitting to do something, making use instead of a decree for specific performance. Even this is unusual where personal services are concerned,[22] the award of damages normally being seen as the more appropriate course. On this basis, one might use a Hohfeldian analysis to suggest that, on the constitutional parallel, unless some legitimate ground for breach/secession is established, Scotland has a duty to remain within/no right to secede from the United Kingdom. At the same time, England, has no (legal) power to make Scotland remain, only to exact damages if secession occurs.

Once constitutional law is viewed in isolation from other parts of domestic law, much turns on whether or not the Treaty of Union is regarded as an entrenched part of it. If not, then the existence of any right for Scotland to secede would seem to depend on there being such a right in international law,[23] either despite the existence of the Treaty or as a result of a serious breach of its terms. If, in contrast, the Treaty is regarded as part of our constitutional law, incorporated into it through the Acts of Union, then it may be possible to argue that an implied constitutional right of secession exists. To date, whilst the Scots courts have never yet avoided legislation on the grounds that it is in breach of the terms of the Scottish Act, they have, equally, never declared themselves debarred from taking such a course.[24] This is, however, far from allowing the inference that they would espouse the existence of a right to secede.

One further possibility exists. Although Article I instates the United Kingdom 'for ever after', Article III does not seem to have quite the same note of finality about it. Different considerations may apply, then, where Parliament is concerned. Certainly, another paradox emerges in relation to the possibility of its legal abolition. Those who would deny that the Treaty is an entrenched part of constitutional law have to regard the Acts of Union as statutes like any other. Only the self-referential, and ultimately unconvincing, doctrine that Parliament cannot alienate its own powers stands between these Acts and their total repeal. By contrast, those who do see the Treaty as an entrenched part of the law – amongst whom are also those most likely to be in favour of Scottish self-determination – would have considerable difficulty in evading its provisions. On the former basis, too, secession from the United Kingdom Parliament, given that this need not legally preclude its continuing to function, might be seen merely as a failure by the Scots to avail themselves of a power to participate. Taking the Treaty seriously, however, makes it easier to read in a breach of a duty to participate into its terms.

Whichever view is taken of its status as law, it is significant that Article III specifies merely that 'the United Kingdom of Great Britain be Represented by one and the same Parliament'. Arguably, this does not present a barrier to the constitution of additional parliaments for different parts of the kingdom. That it does not is crucial to those who adhere to the Treaty view but seek 'home rule' rather than 'independence'. Further, on both the quasi-federal and confederal interpretations of the constitutional structure of Great Britain, the unilateral establishment of a Parliament within Scotland purely to deal with Scottish affairs begins to look like a relatively legitimate constitutional option. All that is breached is the convention that those elected to represent the people of England and Wales are allowed to participate in such affairs. This does seem to require, morally at least, the resolution of the West Lothian question in terms of a *quid pro quo*, according to which the Scots cease to participate in English and Welsh affairs and restrict themselves to federal or confederal ones.

Positive Political Morality

Neither international nor domestic law has proved very fruitful as the source of a right to secede, either explicitly or in terms of affording a consistent set of principles by which one might be generated. It is important to ask, however, whether this type of right is afforded by any politico-moral norms identifiable empirically as held by the players on the international or domestic scene. For such positive political morality can operate as a powerful critical morality where the law is concerned. In this context, it is probable that no right to secede can be found at the international level – at least where the players are seen as states. This is not to say that states do not, from time to time, encourage such movements – but only where this would serve their own political purposes. Such activity is discouraged under international law. Further, the world community is clearly equivocal about the existence of such a right. The powerful generally deny one, given that it would operate independently of particular political purposes. At the same time, the voice of the less powerful cannot be altogether ignored. There are many communities scattered across the globe who do espouse such a right as part of their own domestic positive political morality.

Whether or not the Scots do so is a moot point. Having a desire to secede does not demonstrate commitment to a right to this effect. Equally, commitment to the existence of a right to secede does not imply any actual desire to do so. Even if such a correlation were permissible, there is insufficient empirical evidence in either respect. That said, what can be found is a consistently recurring attitude concerning the proper location and use of political power, including a commitment to the ultimate sovereignty of the Scottish people. Vindicating a right to secede can, therefore, be seen as only one option amongst many directed toward allowing the Scots 'freely to determine ... their political status and to pursue their economic, social and cultural development'. Nonetheless, it is a course that becomes a more likely one to be espoused as other options are foreclosed.

Critical arguments

Amongst international lawyers there is a growing body of opinion that wishes neither to treat the right of self-determination as restricted to decolonisation/individual democratic participation on the one hand, nor as allowing for a fragmentation and proliferation of sovereign states on the other. Amongst the ideas being canvassed are certain guarantees of group autonomy within states and the establishment of a right short of secession – namely that to 'renegotiate' constitutional structures. Since attempts to justify their implementation, however, reflect the arguments offered for and against a right to secede, they are most readily understandable in terms of the latter.

Buchheit (1978), for example, offers a utilitarian argument. He maintains that there simply will be demands for self-determination from people within territorial states. It is, therefore, more consonant with the

UN's aims of maintaining international peace and security if it regulates the conditions under which such demands are to be met. So doing involves judging each such demand on its merits, both internal and external, and weighing up the consequences of secession against the costs or benefits of maintaining the status quo. Internally, there must be a group that is both objectively and subjectively distinct – its members having sufficient out of a list of such characteristics as race, religion, language and tradition of their own to make them so distinct and being united by these characteristics in a 'sentiment of solidarity'.[25] In addition, this group must occupy a distinct territory and must be capable of an independent existence after secession. Externally, the disruptive effects on both the remaining state and other states indirectly concerned and on the international order as a whole must be low (Buchheit, 1978, Ch. 4).

On any such utilitarian calculation, there seems no doubt that Scotland would qualify. The Scots are a group that is both objectively and subjectively distinct. They do occupy a distinct territory and are, on most assessments, capable of an independent existence after secession – at least in the context of separate membership of the European Union.[26] In such a context, too, the disruptive effects on the rest of the United Kingdom would be minimised and those on the international order as a whole very limited. Whether the European Union would agree to Scottish membership is, however, a moot point, given the kind of precedent it would create.[27]

Yet while there may be grounds for engaging in this kind of calculation in assessing the merits of individual claims, it is questionable whether the fact that the absence of a right to self-determination constitutes a potential threat to international peace and security is a sufficiently strong basis for the establishment of such a right. There is a potential threat to international peace and security where one state does not calmly accede to another's occupation of it – but no one argues that this should give rise to a 'right to invade'. Also, some of its proponents argue that use of terroristic force by a potential seceder should cast 'doubt upon the group's ability to comport itself in a civilised manner once independent' (Buchheit, 1978, p.236). This point reinforces doubts about a utilitarian approach, since there seems to be an incoherence in treating the use of force as a factor diminishing the merits of a group's claim to self-determination but the potential for its use as the basis for generating the right to which they aspire.

In consequence, it seems important to find a stronger grounding for a right to self-determination than utilitarianism can afford. One such grounding is suggested by Allen Buchanan, who, after reviewing the moral case both for and against a right of secession,[28] argues that most of the moral case against, including the 'threat of anarchy' argument, falls if proper safeguards are introduced, so that the right is understood to be a limited one. A moral right to secede thus exists under certain circumscribed conditions. At their strongest these include '[t]he state's refusal to cease serious injustices it is perpetrating against the seceding group', such injustices including discriminatory redistribution as well as the violation of basic individual civil and political rights (Buchanan, 1991, p.152). A right to secede may also exist if it is necessary for the preservation of the group's culture,[29] but here Buchanan (1991, p.153) requires that:

> (a) the culture in question must really be threatened – at the very least its prospects of demise in the near future must be significantly greater than the risks all other cultures face. (b) Less drastic ways of preserving the culture than secession (e.g. special minority group rights, a looser federalism, constitutional rights of nullification or group veto) must be unavailable or inadequate. (c) The culture in question must meet minimal standards of moral decency ... (d) The seceding group is not seeking independence in order to establish an illiberal state ... (e) Neither the state nor any third party has a valid claim to the seceding territory.

It has to be said that these conditions – (c) and (d), one would hope, apart – provide difficulties for the Scottish case. One may ask whether Scots culture is sufficiently threatened to meet the Buchanan test. Also, less drastic ways of preserving the culture are unavailable only because of the attitude of the present government. And, whilst no third party may have a valid claim to the territory of Scotland, many would argue that one does exist where the British state is concerned.[30]

However, it may be argued that Buchanan (1991, p.108) overplays the importance of territorial title, eliding his own crucial distinction to the effect that 'Territorial sovereignty is best understood as a set of *jurisdictional* powers over territory, conferred upon the state, not as a special kind of property right'. If, as he himself effectively argues, such powers are a form of trusteeship, then the legitimacy of territorial sovereignty is always contingent – and not just on the manner in which it was acquired. If territorial sovereignty can be lost through the perpetration of serious injustices, then it can be lost – though perhaps not quite so readily – on other grounds as well. Buchanan seems to underrate the demands of cultural preservation in this respect.

Harry Beran (1984, p.30) is far less restrictive in his approach. He claims that 'liberalism requires that any territorially concentrated group within a state should be permitted to secede if it wants to and this is morally and practically possible'. He bases this claim on three aspects of liberalism: the value it attaches to freedom; the nature of its theory of popular sovereignty; and one of its presuppositions about legitimate majority rule. According to the first, within an ideal society 'all relationships between sane adults ... should be voluntary' (Beran, 1984, p.24). According to the second:

Since liberalism, in seeing persons as self-governing choosers, is an individualist philosophy, the sovereignty of the people cannot be an essentially collective property which can only be exercised by all citizens of an existing state within eternally immutable borders. Instead, this sovereignty must be composed of the moral rights of individuals to decide their political relationships (Beran, 1984, p.26).

According to the third, a decision as to whether a

group are to (continue to) be one association cannot always be made in a morally binding way by a majority vote among all the group members. Rather, it follows from the arguments from liberty and sovereignty that, if there are separatists, they should be able to specify the territory of the existing state in which a secessionist referendum is to be held (Beran, 1984, p.27).

Beran's (1984, p.28) conclusion is that secession does not require the moral justification afforded by oppression or the existence of a national right to self-determination. It is sufficient 'that it is deeply desired and pursued by adequate political action'. Secession ought, therefore, to be allowed where it is possible, even if it is not desirable in other ways, for example because multi-national states are preferable to mono-national ones. Nonetheless, Beran (1984, pp.30–1) does qualify this claim by suggesting certain circumstances under which the conditions of moral and practical possibility are not met:

The conditions which *may* justify *not* allowing secession could include the following. (1) The group which wishes to secede is not sufficiently large to assume the basic responsibilities of an independent state. (2) It is not prepared to permit sub-groups within itself to secede although such secession is morally and practically possible. (3) It wishes to exploit or oppress a sub-group within itself which cannot secede in turn because of territorial dispersal or other reasons. (4) It occupies an area not on the borders of the existing state so that secession would create an enclave. (5) It occupies an area which is culturally, economically or militarily essential to the existing state. (6) It occupies an area which has a disproportionately high share of the economic resources of the existing state.

Unlike the criteria set by Buchanan, these conditions seem to pose few problems for the Scottish case, apart from the argument that the desire to secede, rather than to renegotiate political structures, is neither deep enough nor pursued by adequate action.

There are, however, certain difficulties with Beran's analysis. Aside from questions about whether liberalism is quite so individualistic a philosophy as he appears to be maintaining, the basis for his qualifying conditions is not clear. Only the requirements of size and territorial concentration really bear on practical possibility. The others would seem to involve issues of morality. It must be asked whether they, too, can be grounded in liberalism or whether they are generated by a different, and possibly rival, set of principles.

The need to look at secession in context

Tempting though it might be to opt for one of the critical approaches outlined above on the basis of a preference either for its philosophical presuppositions or for its outcome, each seems to raise almost as many questions as it resolves. Part of the reason for this may be that the arguments are not adequately placed within the context of the more general right to self-determination, of which the right to secede is only one form.

Thus, following Beran's line, one might wish to draw further conclusions out of the nature of liberal society. One may begin with the individual. In this case, a consideration of individual autonomy reveals that it is restricted but at the same time socially protected in two different ways, only one of which is through participation in collective processes. The other is through a reserved sphere of individual decision-making, variously constituted as rights and liberties. If, then, we agree with Joxerramon Bengoetxea (1991, p.138) that '[s]elf-determination is a democratic principle which extends the principle of personal moral autonomy to the collective level', it is clearly not enough to ensure that the group, through its members, participates in higher-level collective processes. Consideration must be given to the sphere in which the group may decide for itself – that is to the appropriate extent of self-determination and to the conditions for its effectiveness.[31]

Alternatively one may begin with the group, and look at the value of cultural preservation as well as that of autonomy. The former, it is argued, can be found in the importance of the membership of the group for individual identity and of the group's cultural prosperity for individual development.[32] The latter is looked on as something generated within the group rather than restricted by it. If we accept that the individual has an interest in her or his own personality, then the quality and character of the norms of the group become seen as crucial to its fulfilment. We may wish, therefore, to argue for rights such as those of privacy and freedom of association. But it also becomes possible to argue for a right not to be subject to alien cultural determination.

Various points need to be made about such a right. First, it provides a normative content for the right to self-determination which not only accounts for its strength in the case of salt water colonisations but which can be extended, though perhaps more weakly, to other cases. Second, it cannot be thought to be an absolute right – it must take its place in competition with other 'universal' rights. Third, the group is regarded as a means to an end, not an end in itself. When this approach is applied at state level, the principle of territorial integrity in international law is given its proper context. It is there to prevent individual states from increasing their cultural spheres: not to preclude them from being diminished. Fourth, the right is one that becomes operative at the lowest possible level. In general terms, this seems to lead in the direction of Paul Hirst's (1994) 'associative democracy'.

One final point is, however, worth making. Many of the difficulties placed in the way of those who wish to argue for the existence of a right to secede rest upon particular (and outdated) notions of state and law. As various trends in international law suggest and as Neil MacCormick (1993) has powerfully argued, we have already moved 'Beyond the Sovereign State'. Yet secession is itself usually understood as involving a bid to form such a state. The two positions cannot readily be equated. To this extent, discussion of the nature of a right to secede is putting the cart before the horse. Also – as it is to the nature of the right to self-determination that we should look first – we may ask why the onus should not be on those who would limit it to justify their position. In which case, the issues might be explored again under a different title, namely: 'A right to the status quo? The United Kingdom reviewed'.

Notes

1 This paper deals only with issues of political and not economic self-determination, although the two cannot be entirely separated, as the slogan 'It's Scotland's Oil' makes clear. Also, for sake of simplicity, the paper makes no mention of Wales or Ireland. In consequence, the term 'United Kingdom' is mainly used to refer to Great Britain, although in some contexts it should be read as Great Britain and Northern Ireland.

2 That is, a right to a particular form of self-determination involving the assertion of jurisdiction over territory that currently falls within the boundaries of an existing state (Buchanan, 1991, p.10).

3 In Article 1 (2) one of the purposes of the UN is stated as being '[t]o develop friendly relations among nations based on respect for the principles of equal rights and of self-determination of peoples, ...'

4 'The General Assembly ... Declares that:

　1 The subjection of peoples to alien subjugation, domination and exploitation constitutes a denial of fundamental human rights, is contrary to the Charter of the United Nations and is an impediment to the promotion of world peace and co-operation;

2 All peoples have the right to self-determination; by virtue of that right they freely determine their political status and freely pursue their economic, social and cultural development; ...'

5 These are not meant to be exhaustive and are, anyway, 'ideal types'. It is sometimes difficult to decide into which of them particular examples should be placed.

6 The last four possibilities become further complicated by the question of whether the people concerned still occupy a distinct part of the territory or are scattered throughout it and, if the former, where this territory falls in relation to the boundaries of the state as a whole.

7 As, for example, Canada, with the British North America Act 1867, until the repatriation of the Constitution in 1982.

8 As with that of France Outre-mer in the French Parliament.

9 Both for the sorts of reasons offered by Buchheit (1978, pp.21–2) and because it is an inappropriate use of the principle of the territorial integrity of states.

10 There are of course many individuals south of Scotland who would claim to be Scottish and/or who would be accepted as such on objective criteria and, equally, many who form part of the population of Scotland who would not. Nonetheless, since there is a clearly defined territorial area that would be involved in the exercise of any right of secession and, since those living in that area can be claimed to be doing so under a separately identifiable set of cultural norms, it seems permissible to make the equation in this context.

11 With certain permissible exceptions.

12 The Constitutional Convention has, for example, proposed what is essentially a federal arrangement.

13 Such as for Palestine and for South Africa before the recent reforms.

14 Buchheit (1978, pp.28–30) identifies these as fears of: Balkanisation; indefinite divisibility; the effect on the democratic system; infirm states; 'trapped' minorities; 'stranded' majorities.

15 Self-determination is, thus, being regarded as a principle of inclusion, not exclusion.

16 That it cannot do so successfully can be shown by substituting the term 'nation' for 'peoples', at which point it becomes evident that, in representing the people of a state as a nation, an attempt is being made to paint a particular picture – that of a homogeneous community. This operates to deny the possibility of the right to self-determination, seen as an exclusionary right, belonging anywhere than in the community/nation/state as a whole. Similarly, as an inclusionary right, it functions only on the level of individual democratic participation since, in a homogeneous community, nothing more is needed. This particular picture fails to convince, simply because modern states are rarely homogeneous in this way.

17 This leads some writers, such as Buchanan (1991, p.67ff) to see one of the strongest cases for such a right being made out where there has been 'unjust incorporation'.

18 E.g. the Toleration Act 1712 (otherwise the Scottish Episcopalians Act 1711).

19 And, occasionally, it may be added, Scottish and English law.

20 See, particularly, the discussion of Müllerson (1994).

21 *White and Carter (Councils) Ltd v. McGregor* 1962 SC (HL) 1, overturning *Langford v. Dutch* 1952 SC 15.

22 French law, for example, allowing only damages in such cases.

23 Unlike the law of contract, however, the lack of a right to secede would not here necessarily imply a duty not to do so.

24 Beginning with *Mackenzie v Stewart* (1752) M 7443, through a series of cases of which the most recent is *Pringle, Petitioner* 1991 SLT 332.

25 *The Greco-Bulgarian 'Communities'* Case [1920] PCIJ., ser B No 17, at 33, quoted in Buchheit (1978, p.229).

26 To this extent the Scottish National Party slogan of 'Independence in Europe' is not altogether an oxymoron.

27 Opposition might, for example, come from Spain and France, given the possible effects for their Basque populations.

28 He devotes considerably more space to the case for (approximately 53 pages) than to the case against (approximately 36), demonstrating the latter's limited applicability and placing strict limitations on any right to resist actual secession by force.

29 Or for the literal survival of the group's members, where the state is not adequately protecting them against a third party aggressor.

30 In this respect Scotland is worse placed than, for example, Quebec, because of the voluntary nature of the Treaty and Acts of Union, by comparison with the acquisition of Quebec by conquest from the French.

31 These may include no, some or near-monopolistic jurisdictional powers over territory.

32 Such ideas may be found amongst the writings of Kymlicka (1989), to whom Buchanan adverts; of Margalit and Raz (1990); Miller (1993); and MacMurray (1957 and 1961).

References

Bentham, Jeremy (1967), *A Fragment on Government*, Blackwell: Oxford.

Beran, Harry (1984), 'A Liberal Theory of Secession', *Political Studies*, Vol. 32, pp.21–31.

Bengoetxea, Joxerramon (1991), 'Nationality and Self-Determination: The Basque Case' in Twining, William (ed.), *Issues in Self-Determination*, Aberdeen University Press: Aberdeen.

Buchanan, Allen (1991), *Secession: The Morality of Political Divorce from Fort Sumter to Lithuania and Quebec*, Westview Press: Oxford.

Buchheit, Lee C. (1978), *Secession: The Legitimacy of Self-Determination*, Yale University Press: New Haven and London.

Ewin, R.E. (1994), 'Peoples and Secession', *Journal of Applied Philosophy*, Vol. 11, No. 2, pp.225–31.

Hirst, Paul (1994), *Associative Democracy*, Polity Press: Oxford.

Kymlicka, Will (1989), *Liberalism, Community and Culture*, Oxford University Press: Oxford.

MacCormick, Neil (1993), 'Beyond the Sovereign State', *Modern Law Review*, 56, pp.1–19.

MacMurray, John (1957), *The Self as Agent*, Faber: London.

MacMurray, John (1961), *Persons in Relation*, Faber: London.

Margalit, Avishai and Raz, Joseph (1990), 'National Self-Determination', *Journal of Philosophy*, Vol. LXXXVII, No. 9, pp.439–61.

Miller, David (1993), 'In Defence of Nationality', *Journal of Applied Philosophy*, Vol. 10, No. 1, pp.3–16.

Müllerson, Rein (1994), *International Law, Rights and Politics*, Routledge: London.

Nielsen, Kai (1993), 'Secession: The Case of Quebec', *Journal of Applied Philosophy*, Vol. 10, No. 1, pp.29–43.

Secretariat of the International Commission of Jurists (1972), 'The Events in East Pakistan, 1971'.

Upton, Michael (1989), 'Marriage Vows of the Elephant: The Constitution of 1707', *Law Quarterly Review*, 105, pp.79–103.

10 Beyond sovereignty and citizenship: a global constitutionalism

Luigi Ferrajoli

Introduction: sovereignty, citizenship and the state

The traditional meanings of sovereignty and citizenship have been called into question by the total crisis of the nation state to which they are both linked: the first insofar as it designates the state's complete independence from internal and external judicial bonds; the second insofar as it represents the subjective status of membership of a given political community. The thesis that I will develop here is that the changes associated with this crisis cannot be interpreted as bringing into being new kinds of sovereignty and citizenship. Rather, they have resulted in a paradigm shift within international law and its framing of the rights of states. This shift has overturned the old categories of the state-centred view of law, giving rise to deep antinomies between the accepted notions of sovereignty and citizenship on the one side and constitutionalism and human rights on the other. In fact, the concepts of sovereignty and citizenship continue to inform the relations of cohabitation and conflict, inclusion and exclusion which pertain amongst states and between peoples and persons. Nonetheless, both these notions have not only lost much of their effectiveness and legitimacy as the means of providing internal peace, political integration and guaranteeing fundamental rights, but are also at odds with what I shall call the constitutional paradigm that informs both the idea of the *Rechtsstaat* and the current understanding of international law.

Sovereignty, citizenship and domestic constitutional law

The first antinomy I wish to explore concerns the relationship between sovereignty and domestic public law. The history of sovereignty as, in Bodin's (1962) classic definition 'potestas legibus soluta' incorporates two parallel and opposed developments. The history of internal sovereignty involves its progressive dissolution with the formation of democratic and constitutional states. The history of external sovereignty involves its progressive concentration, a process reaching its apogee in the first half of this century with the catastrophes of the two world wars. The first history begins with the end of monarchical absolutism and the birth of the liberal state. The French declaration of rights of 1789 and the constitutions that followed changed the nature of the state and with it the principle of internal sovereignty. The division of powers, the principle of legality and fundamental rights represented so many limitations and, in the last analysis, negations of internal sovereignty, that the relationship between state and citizen was transformed into one between two subjects possessing limited sovereignty.

Within 19th century conceptions of the liberal state an element of absolutism remained in the legal positivist conception of the supremacy of law and the omnipotence of parliament as the agency of popular sovereignty. But even this remaining element was diminished with the invention in our century of rigid constitutions and judicial control of the constitutionality of laws. The legal positivist and 'democratic' doctrine of the omnipotence of the legislature and the sovereignty of parliament was then shattered and replaced by the idea of the *Rechtsstaat*, according to which even the legislative power of the majority is subject to constitutional law. Within constitutional democracies absolute and sovereign powers or subjects no longer exist. The very principle of popular sovereignty that is still included in many constitutions is no more than a verbal homage to the democratic-representative character of contemporary political systems.

In contrast, the principle of external sovereignty has followed a trajectory moving in precisely the opposite direction. International society, which at the beginning of the modern era Francisco de Vitoria (1934), Alberico Gentili (1933) and Hugo Grotius (1925) had conceived of as a society of free and independent republics subject to the same fundamental human law, came to be seen by contractualist political philosophy as a savage society still in the state of nature. According to writers such as Hobbes (1991) and Locke (1960), states found themselves in the condition of *bellum omnium*: a natural and not simply a purely theoretical condition, such as it was imagined might once have existed between human beings before the formation of political societies. In Hobbes' (1991, p.149) words:

> in States, and Common-wealths not dependent on one another, every Common-wealth, ... has an absolute libertie, to doe what it shall judge (that is to say, what that Man, or Assemblie that representeth it, shall judge) most conducing to their benefit. But withall, they live in the condition of a perpetuall war, and upon the confines of battel, with their frontiers armed, and canons planted against their neighbours round about.

152

The overcoming of the state of nature within and its conservation (or establishment) without became in this way the two lines of development along which the history of modern states unfolded, both of which were inscribed in their genetic code by the political philosophy of the natural law tradition. The modern state is a sovereign subject that is consequently based on two opposing principles – the negation and the affirmation of the state of nature. It negates the state of nature insofar as the civil state is opposed to the natural state of man red in tooth and claw and civilisation is contrasted with barbarism as a legitimating source of new types of inequality and domination. The modern state affirms the state of nature as a consequence of the savage but artificial society existing amongst sovereign states, which are in a virtual condition of war amongst each other but are also united, as the 'civilised world', by the right-cum-duty to civilise the remaining 'barbaric' parts of the world.

These two opposed trends reached their fullest development in the last century and the beginning of the present one. While the liberal democratic nation-state was based internally on the subjection of all public powers to the rule of law and popular representation, it freed itself in its external relations from all legal limits. The two processes were simultaneous and paradoxically connected. The state under law within and the absolute state without grew up together as the two sides of the same coin. The more the state limited its internal sovereignty and gained in legitimacy through having imposed these limits upon itself, the more external sovereignty became absolute and legitimate with regard to other states – particularly so far as the uncivilised world was concerned. The more the state of nature was overcome within, the more it developed without. And the more the state developed as a legal order, the more it was able to affirm itself as a self-sufficient entity, identified with the law but, precisely because of this, not subject to the law.

This phenomenon gives rise to a second antinomy: that existing between the universalism of fundamental rights and their state-bound realisation through citizenship. In spite of the fact that these rights, with the exception of the political ones, are always proclaimed to be universal, from the Declaration of the Rights of Man of 1789 onwards, through all the succeeding constitutions and even in civil codes ('the exercise of civil rights' established by Article 7 of the Napoleonic Code, for example, is declared to be 'independent of the status of citizenship'), the judicial 'universe' has ended up coinciding with the internal order of each and every state. This antinomy has come to light in recent years with the explosion of immigration. These rights were proclaimed universal when the distinction between man and citizen did not create any problems, it being neither likely or foreseeable that the men and women of the third world would arrive in Europe and that these statements of principle might be taken literally. If anything during the past two centuries the opposite has occurred – namely the invasion and colonisation of the rest of the world by Europeans: in support of which, it is worth remembering, both the *ius migrandi* and the *ius accipiendi civitatem* were theorised almost five centuries ago by Francesco de Vitoria (1934) as the most basic natural rights of human beings.

Today the universalism of human rights is put to the test by the pressure placed on our borders by hoards of starving people, as a result of which to be a person has ceased to be a sufficient condition for possessing these rights. They have come to be, following the by now classic thesis of T.H. Marshall (1950), 'rights of citizenship'. Indeed, citizenship has become the prerequisite of the right of entry and residence in the territory of the state. In this way, citizenship has ceased to be the foundation of equality. While internally citizenship has fractured into different types of unequal citizenship corresponding to new differentiations of status that range from full citizens to semi-citizens with the right of residence, refugees and illegal immigrants, externally citizenship functions as a privilege and a source of exclusion and discrimination with regard to non-citizens.

Sovereignty and citizenship within the new international law: a global constitutionalism

With the birth of the United Nations this antinomy between the traditional concepts of sovereignty and citizenship, on the one hand, and the domestic law of constitutional states, on the other, has arisen at the level of international law as well. Both the principle of external sovereignty and the idea of citizenship as a presupposition of human rights are at odds with both the United Nations Charter of 1945 and the Universal Declaration of Rights of Man of 1948.

At least at a normative level, these two documents transformed the legal order of the world, taking it from the state of nature to the civil state. The signatory states were legally subject to fundamental norms: the imperative of peace and the maintenance of human rights. From that moment sovereignty became a logically inconsistent concept. On the one hand, the prohibition against war upheld by the United Nations Charter overruled the *ius ad bellum* that had always been its main attribute. On the other hand, the sanctification of human rights in the Declaration of 1948 and the treaties of 1966 made them not only constitutional rights but also supra-state rights, transforming them into external and not simply internal limits on the power of states. A paradigm shift has occurred within international law, changing it from a contractual system based on bilateral and equal relations between sovereign states into a true legal order of a supra-state kind.

At this point sovereignty, which had already been emptied of any real content in its internal dimension with the development of the constitutional state, was also diminished in its external dimension, finally revealing itself to be a category that is incompatible with law. We can now affirm that its crisis both internally and externally began from the moment in which it entered into relation with law. For the attributes of sovereignty – namely the absence of limits and of rules – render it the negation of law and vice versa.

The idea of citizenship as a presupposition of rights collapsed at the same time, at least at a juridical level. This idea was in contradiction with the universalism of rights at the level of both domestic and international law. If legal subjectivity consists in being a rights bearer and citizenship entails that one can only claim rights through belonging to a given political community, in the new paradigm every human being is already a subject of international law and so is a citizen not only of a given state but also of the international communities, be they regional in nature, such as the European Union, or of a global character, as with the United Nations.

Naturally, this transformation has occurred almost solely at the legal normative level. So far as actual international relations are concerned, both the principle of sovereignty and the exclusive view of citizenship still hold sway. But sovereignty is by now nothing more than a legal black hole, its rule being the absence of rules, in other words the law of the strongest. So far as citizenship is concerned, it has become the last personal privilege, the last factor of discrimination and the last relic of pre-modern differences in status; as such it is opposed to the acclaimed universality and equality of fundamental rights.

This paradigm shift allows us to see a complex of antinomies and lacunas in the notions of sovereignty and citizenship: antinomies between both the new normative principles of peace and justice and the avoidance of them by the enduring sovereignty of states and between the universalism of rights and the continuing exclusive nature of citizenship; lacunas in the absence of effective instruments capable of guaranteeing and securing the practical efficacy of the new paradigm and of remedying its continued violation and denial.

To recognise these antinomies between the principles of sovereignty and citizenship, on the one side, and the new paradigm of international law, on the other, is to 'take seriously', in Ronald Dworkin's (1978) apt phrase, the existing international legal framework. It is to recognise the global constitution in embryo which already exists in the United Nations Charter and the various international conventions and declarations of human rights. It involves viewing reality from the vantage point of a global constitutionalism that has already been formally established, even if it is still lacking any institutional guarantees. More particularly, it involves conceiving of war, oppression, threats to the environment and the condition of hunger and misery in which thousands of people live, not as natural evils or even as simple injustices but as legal violations of the principles inscribed in those charters as binding norms of positive law. It also means seeing the absence of guarantees, in the sense of instruments capable of enforcing these rights, not as something that renders these rights worthless but as an improper lacuna that we have an obligation to fill. As the French constitution of the Year Three put it: 'The declaration of rights contains within it the duties of legislatures'. This statement sums up the essence of constitutionalism.

Three issues for a global constitutionalism

A global constitutionalism raises three main issues for legal theory: (a) the *absence of judicial guarantees* at an international level; (b) the *shift of the loci of constitutional guarantees* following on from the weakening of state sovereignty; (c) the possibility of a *right to asylum* as a counter-weight, however weak, to the statist view of fundamental rights deriving from citizenship.

(a) The main lacuna within the global constitutional paradigm of international law is the absence of judicial guarantees in support of peace and human rights. It is to such guarantees, rather than to an unlikely and not even desirable global government, that 50 years ago Kelsen (1944) entrusted the role of limiting the sovereignty of states. Such a lacuna is usually explained by referring to the lack of an international authority with the monopoly of force – the 'absent third' as Bobbio (1989) calls it. However, this argument underestimates the availability of economic and other non-violent sanctions. More importantly, it also overlooks the political authority and legitimacy that, in the long run, an independent Court's decisions would derive through being grounded in such universally supported laws as those established to defend peace and human rights, particularly in an age of mass communications.

Existing international legal institutions are of limited value in this new situation. In contrast to the current International Court of Justice, whose jurisdiction is limited to controversies between states and only applies if recognised by the states themselves, an international tribunal guaranteeing peace and human rights should broaden its competencies to decide both on the constitutionality of the United Nations deliberations and on responsibilities in matters of war, threats to peace and violations of human rights. These decisions should no longer take the form of arbitration, but ought to consist of judgments that are binding on all the parties concerned. Unlike the special tribunal for war crimes committed in the former Yugoslavia, this new international tribunal should not operate ex-post, but as a permanent institution. International crimes – such as war, permanent damage to the environment, and grave violations of human rights – should be fixed in advance and listed in an international penal code.

(b) The second issue I wish to highlight concerns the difficulty of establishing a hierarchy amongst the sources of law. This problem is present within any constitutional paradigm. However, it arises with a particular urgency when processes of international integration reach an advanced stage, as the European Union illustrates. The displacement of decision-making away from nation states of matters which had previously been reserved to their sovereign power, such as defence and monetary and social policy, alters the whole system of legal sources and in the process risks weakening the authority of national constitutions. One has only to think of the supra-legal value currently attributed to the sources of European law – directives, European Community regulations and, after Maastricht, economic and military decisions – all of which issue from bodies that are subject neither to the control of national parliaments nor to constitutional constraints. It is evident that, in so far as they prevail over the laws and even the constitutions of the member states, these new normative sources risk upsetting the constitutional structure of European democracies and open up new opportunities for a revived neo-absolutism.

This new situation calls for a rethinking of constitutionalism. It underlines the need to devise constitutional guarantees of peace and human rights not just at a national but also at a supra-national level, that are capable of controlling the agencies that increasingly *de facto* take a whole range of vital decisions without being politically accountable and in the absence of any constitutional controls. Nowadays, because of the irrationality of its institutional structure, the European Union in particular is a political actor that operates without a constitution. It possesses a Parliament with consultative and controlling, but no legislative functions; a Council of Ministers with normative functions, but which is free from parliamentary control; a Commission with administrative functions, but which are largely independent from those of the Council; and a Court of Justice with many, but largely irrelevant competencies.

The sole democratic foundation of the unity and cohesion of a political system is its constitution, and the type of allegiance it alone can generate – the so called 'constitutional patriotism' (Habermas, 1992). For this very reason, it seems to me that the future of Europe as a political entity depends to a great extent on developing a constituent process open to public debate, aimed at framing a *European constitution*. This constitution should provide criteria of validity that are strictly superior to the national and community sources of law and should guarantee universal human rights, independently of the requirements of citizenship.

(c) The third issue concerns the migratory pressure which endless masses are placing on western nations. Because they do not qualify for citizenship, the vital rights of these migrants are denied and they are condemned to a sort of *apartheid*. One should note that this is not a transitory phenomenon, but one which will grow exponentially in the near future. In the long term, because of its unsustainable and explosive nature, the antinomy between the universality of rights and citizenship will be solved only by the *overcoming of citizenship* and the *denationalisation* of human rights. However, it is clear that if we are gradually to move towards a universal

157

citizenship while at the same time providing some more immediate solutions to a problem that has already become the greatest currently facing humanity, then the right to asylum must be extended and not, as is presently occurring, made increasingly restrictive.

The right to asylum suffers from the defect of being, so to speak, the other side of the coin of citizenship and sovereignty and the state-centred conception they offer of fundamental rights. Traditionally, it has been restricted to people subject to political, racial and religious persecution, and has not applied to refugees whose rights to subsistence have been infringed. This limitation reflects a paleo-liberal phase of constitutionalism, in which, on the one hand, the only recognised rights were political rights and those based on negative liberties and, on the other, economic migration occurred largely between western states, notably from European countries to North and South America, and to their mutual benefit.

Matters are very different today. In addition to the classical rights of negative liberty, contemporary European constitutions and international charters of rights now recognise a long list of positive human rights – not just to life and liberty, but also to subsistence and survival. These rights are not grounded in citizenship and they too form the basis of modern notions of legal equality and of the dignity of the human person. There is no reason why protection should not also cover grave violation of these other rights and be extended to economic as well as political refugees. Indeed, this policy follows directly on from Articles 13 and 14 of the Universal Declaration of 1948 which deal with the freedom of movement within 'every state'.

Instead, at present the restrictive thesis seems to prevail, as a consequence of tougher immigration laws and of their more rigid application, or, even worse, of their tacit violation. This policy results in the closure of the West. It risks both undermining the universalistic design of the United Nations and deforming our democracies through the creation of a regressive European identity, cemented around hatred of 'the other' and by what Habermas has called 'welfare chauvinism'. In fact, there is a close link between democracy and equality, on the one hand, and between inequality of rights and racism, on the other. Just as parity of rights generates a sense of equality based on respect for the other as an equal, so inequality of entitlements produces an image of the other as different, as some one who must be anthropologically inferior because legally so.

Short- and long-term realism: the role of legal science

The universalising project enshrined in the United Nations Charter's guarantees of peace and the equal entitlement to fundamental rights of all human beings is most commonly criticised for being utopian. Even though it has a basis in existing international law, such a project is said to be impractical because it flies in the face of the power relations that have always dominated history.

This opposition between realism and utopianism misdescribes the situation. The real distinction is between short- and long-term realism. The most unrealistic hypothesis is to imagine that reality will indefinitely remain as it is, that we may indefinitely fund our rich democracies and comfortable and carefree standards of life by starvation and misery in the rest of the world. Realistically, none of this can last. Although perhaps unrealistic in the short term, as demonstrated by the many recent failures of the United Nations, the legal project at the basis of global constitutionalism is, in the long term, the only realistic alternative to war, destruction, the rise of a variety of fundamentalisms, ethnic conflicts, terrorism, an increase in famines and general misery. After the failure of the revolutionary utopias of this century, which were based on the 'realistic' devaluation of the system of law, it ought to be recognised that there is no realistic alternative to the rule of law. After all, even political realism is founded on a legal utopia: namely, the belief that domestic laws can stem the pressure of the excluded at the national frontiers. As is always the case when the law is deployed to stop a mass phenomenon (like abortion or drugs, for instance) the only result is to render it clandestine and to draw the people involved in it towards crime. Indeed, the preamble of the Declaration of 1948 identifies the violation of human rights as the principal cause of war and violence.

The preceding argument suggests that philosophical and legal culture have an important duty. There is an epistemological paradox at the heart of these disciplines. We are part of the universe we describe, and contribute, perhaps more than we are aware, to making it. How the system of law *is* and how it *will be* also depends on the prevailing legal culture. This is the more so if we wish constitutional and international law to be taken seriously. Legal science has never limited itself to the study and commentary of how law is, nor to how it should be developed. Legal science has always produced *images* of law and of legal order, which imply a shared sense of the reasons for political obedience. This was true of the *Rechtsstaat* and remains so of our still-fragile democracies. There is no reason to believe that it will be any different for international law, especially given that the new paradigm of the primacy and guarantee of human rights as the conditions for world peace and coexistence reflects the growing expectations and the common sense of people as they become gradually more aware of the increase in global interdependence.

References

Bobbio, N. (1989), *Il terzo assente: Saggi sulla pace e sulla guerra*, Edizioni Sonda: Turin.

Bodin, J. (1962), *The Six Bookes of a Commonweale*, first edition 1576, trans. R. Knowles, McRae, K.D. (ed.), Harvard University Press: Cambridge, Mass.

Dworkin, R. (1978), *Taking Rights Seriously*, Duckworth: London.

Gentili, A. (1933), *De iure belli libri tres*, first edition 1588, intro. C. Phillipson, 2 vols., Clarendon Press: Oxford.

Grotius, H. (1925), *De Jure Belli ac Pacis libri tres*, first edition 1646, Classics of International Law, Clarendon Press: Oxford.

Habermas, J. (1992), 'Citizenship and National Identity: Some Reflections on the Future of Europe', *Praxis International*, Vol. 12, No. 1, pp.1–19.

Hobbes, T. (1991), *Leviathan*, first edition 1651, Tuck, Richard (ed.), Cambridge University Press: Cambridge.

Kelsen, H. (1944), *Peace Through Law*, University of North Carolina Press: Chapel Hill.

Locke, J. (1960), *Two Treatises of Government*, first edition 1689, Laslett, P. (ed.), Cambridge University Press: Cambridge.

Marshall, T.H. (1950), *Citizenship and Social* Class, Cambridge University Press: Cambridge.

Vitoria, Francisco de (1934), *De Indis Recenter Inventis*, first edition in (1539) *Relecciones Teologicas del Maestro Fray Francisco de Vitoria*, Getino, L.G.A. (ed.), La Rafa: Madrid, Vol. 2, pp.281–438.

Contributors

John Arthur is Professor of Law and Director of the programme in philosophy, politics and law at Binghamton, SUNY. He is the author of *The Unfinished Constitution* (1989), *Words that Bind: Judicial Review and the Grounds of Modern Constitutional Theory* (1995) and co-editor of *Campus Wars: Multi-culturalism and the Politics of Difference* (1995).

Elspeth Attwooll is Senior Lecturer in Jurisprudence at the University of Glasgow. She teaches legal theory and comparative law and has a special interest in the theory of international law. She is currently involved in editing and contributing to collections of essays in these areas.

Zenon Bankowski is Professor of Legal Theory in the Centre of Criminology and the Social and Philosophical Study of Law at the University of Edinburgh. His research interests are in the legal theory of the European Union, legal reasoning, law, social theory and theology. He is co-author of *Lay Justice?* (1987) and co-editor of *Informatics and the Foundations of Legal Reasoning* (1995).

Richard Bellamy was Professor of Politics in the School of Economic and Social Studies at the University of East Anglia and is now Professor of Politics at the University of Reading. He is the author of, amongst other works, *Liberalism and Modern Society* (1992), co-author of *Gramsci and the Italian State* (1993) and co-editor of *Democracy and Constitutional Culture in the Union of Europe* (1995) and *The Constitution in Transformation* (1996).

Dario Castiglione is Lecturer in Political Theory at the University of Exeter. He is the author of articles on the history of 18th century political philosophy and on theories of civil society, and co-editor of *Democracy* *and Constitutional Culture in the Union of Europe* (1995), *Shifting Boundaries: The Transformation of the Languages of Public and Private in the Eighteenth Century* (1995) and *The Constitution in Transformation* (1996).

Luigi Ferajoli is Professor of Law and Legal Theory at the University of Camerino. From 1967–75 he acted as a judge. He is the author of *Diritto e ragione. Teoria del garantismo penale* (second edition 1990) and *La Sovranità nel mondo moderno* (1995).

Vivien Hart is Reader in American Studies at the University of Sussex. She is the author of *Distrust and Democracy: Political Distrust in Britain and America* (1978), *Bound by our Constitution: Women, Workers and Minimum Wage Laws* (1994) and co-editor of *Writing a National Identity: Political, Economic and Cultural Perspectives on the Written Constitution* (1993).

Elizabeth Kingdom is Senior Lecturer in Sociology at the University of Liverpool. She is the author of *What's Wrong with Rights?: Problems for Feminist Politics of Law* (1991) and co-editor of *Women's Rights and the Rights of Man* (1991).

Carole Lyons is the Jean Monnet Lecturer in Law and Politics of European Integration at the University of East Anglia. She is the author of articles on the rights of immigrants and citizenship in the European Union.

Ulrich K. Preuss is Professor of Constitutional and Administrative Law, Director of the Zentrum für Europäische Rechtspolitik at the University of Bremen and a member of the Constitutional Court of the Land of Bremen. He is the author of numerous publications, including *Constitutional Revolution: The Link Between Constitutionalism and Progress* (1995) and (with Jon Elster and Claus Offe) *Constitutional and Economic Transitions in Eastern Europe* (1996). He is currently directing a major research project on European Citizenship.

Andrew Scott is Jean Monnet Senior Lecturer in the Economics of the European Union at the Europa Institute, University of Edinburgh. He has published widely on issues relating to European economic integration. He is joint editor of the *Journal of Common Market Studies*.

162